A HORSE IN YOUR BACKYARD?

A HORSE IN YOUR BACKYARD?

BY

VIRGINIA PHELPS CLEMENS

THE WESTMINSTER PRESS

PHILADELPHIA

BOOK DESIGN BY DOROTHY ALDEN SMITH

First Edition

Published by The Westminster Press®
Philadelphia, Pennsylvania

PRINTED IN THE UNITED STATES OF AMERICA

1 2 3 4 5 6 7 8 9

PHOTO CREDITS: Standard Photo Service, p. 116; all others, Virginia Clemens
DRAWINGS BY: Thomas Forcey

Library of Congress Cataloging in Publication Data

Clemens, Virginia Phelps.
A horse in your backyard?

Bibliography: p.
Includes index.
SUMMARY: Discusses the selection and care of a young rider's first horse.
1. Horses—Juvenile literature. [1. Horses.
2. Horsemanship] I. Title.
SF302.C58   636.1'08   77-7394
ISBN 0-664-32616-1

For Doug,
    whose patience and understanding
    helped to make this book possible,
and for our children,
Ted, Greg, and Shari

CONTENTS

INTRODUCTION

Is there a horse in your backyard? Or are you planning to take up horsekeeping in the near future?

If so, you must have numerous questions, and possibly no one to answer them.

Information included in this book, from horse owners, stable managers, veterinarians, blacksmiths, feed dealers, and tack shop owners, should answer all your questions and quite probably many you never considered.

Congratulations for trying to find out the best way to care for your new pet. Unfortunately, too many horse owners, old and new, take for granted that their horses will do quite well with no more care than they give their dog or cat. After all, the mustangs on the plains have no one to feed, groom, or clean up after them.

Horses suffer in silence. Through ignorance, carelessness, selfishness, and even an overabundance of kindness at the wrong time—rarely deliberate cruelty—too many do suffer.

Even the horse experts have a variety of opinions and methods on caring, selecting, training, and riding a horse. To use a hay net or hayrack, or just to throw the hay in a corner of the stall? To keep a halter on the horse when he is in the barn or out in the pasture? What feed and bedding do the best job? Knowledgeable horse owners still disagree.

A HORSE IN YOUR BACKYARD? offers logical and easy-to-follow advice and hints for the young horse owner with his or her first horse. But you must decide for yourself what works best with your horse and is most convenient for you. What agrees with the majority of equines may not be the ideal method for your pet, so experiment a little, using the information in this book as a starting point.

1
PROS AND CONS
OF BACKYARD HORSEKEEPING

Probably you have been a horse lover ever since you read *Misty of Chincoteague,* saw a TV cowboy gallop off into the sunset, or were allowed to feed a few blades of grass, roots and all, to some soft-lipped dobbin stretching his head over a pasture fence.

One of the most popular sports in the United States today, horseback riding is also one of the most healthful—providing fresh air and vigorous exercise for its enthusiasts.

In 1960 there were three million riding horses in this country. In 1973 the Department of Agriculture estimated that there were six million, and by 1978, horse breeders predict that the horse population in the United States will climb to over ten million.

KNOW YOUR OBLIGATIONS

Whether you've just persuaded your parents into becoming a horse-owning family or are still trying to point out the value of a large pet, you should be aware of the responsibilities and just plain hard work it takes to keep a horse. You must have plenty of patience and be willing to perform dirty, sometimes exhausting chores.

Although horses are relatively cheap to buy, their upkeep can become quite a financial burden. Monthly payments for food and board, services of a blacksmith and veterinarian, and cost of equipment (saddle, blankets, brushes, pails, etc.) mount up quickly and considerably.

Adult supervision is a must, no matter how mature and dependable you are. A horse needs regular daily attention and other family members should be willing to help you. Although you vow to take care of your horse all by yourself, emergencies will occur. In fact, a horse in the backyard is a hobby and an experience that the whole family should want to share.

A horse in the backyard is a hobby that the whole family should want to share

Your parents should realize that after the novelty of owning a horse wears off, you may need a little reminding of your obligation in the backyard. Such deterrents as the wind-chill factor, homework piled high on the kitchen table, or an invitation to an upcoming party will just have to wait until those stable chores are finished.

PREPARATIONS FOR HORSEKEEPING

Before buying a horse you should take riding lessons from a qualified instructor. Learning to ride by yourself in your backyard or along a nearby trail is hardly the safest thing to do.

Learn to ride English style rather than Western. If you know how to ride English, you can easily switch to Western, but those riding Western are usually lost on an English trained and tacked horse.

Knowing how to ride is only part of what's needed to keep your horse healthy and happy. How to care for him properly is important too.

If you have had little hands-on experience (reading about it is not doing it!) with horses, contact a local riding school and make arrangements for riding lessons. Your neighborhood veterinarian can probably recommend a reliable stable. Lessons often include information about the care of horses, but if yours don't, volunteer to help groom horses, muck out stalls, and clean tack to learn what you will be doing as a horse owner. The stable manager will probably welcome the extra help and you will be gaining valuable

A small child may ride beautifully but will need adult supervision if she is a horse owner

experience. You will also be making a knowledgeable friend to whom you can turn for horse-related advice.

Local 4-H and Pony Clubs are fine organizations to consider joining as another way to meet other horse and pony owners. The 4-H Clubs focus primarily on animal care and urge members to "learn by doing." Once a club has chosen its projects, such as the care of a horse, the members must periodically turn in reports and charts of their daily progress—a good way of having methods of horse care evaluated.

Pony Clubs emphasize all aspects of horsemanship, and especially encourage improvement in riding through rallies, clinics, and a rider rating system. In order to advance to a higher rating, Pony Club members must pass both written and riding tests.

Speakers and demonstrators at meetings of both 4-H and Pony Clubs provide additional information on horsekeeping. Your county agricultural agent and SPCA can also give you advice on caring for a horse in your area.

Applicants for the 4-H Club must be at least nine years old. Depending on the individual, this is a good minimum age for a child to start riding lessons and learning how to care for a horse. However, a few years older, twelve and up, is a more practical age for the chores. A child of five may ride beautifully, but just won't have the physical strength to muck out a stall, properly groom a horse, or even lift the saddle into place.

A possible horse owner should be mature enough to see the work ahead and to have the stick-to-itiveness to keep up with the chores after the newness wears off. You and your family might consider asking your riding instructor for his or her opinion on whether you are ready to take on the responsibility of a horse.

BOARDING

The next step toward keeping a horse in your backyard is to determine whether it is suitable or whether it would be more convenient to board your horse at a local stable.

There are usually two kinds of boarding arrangements. A bare stall is the cheapest arrangement. It includes just the stall—box or straight. A box stall is more expensive but gives the horse room to move about, while a straight stall is narrow (5 × 8 feet) and the horse is tied with just enough room to lie down. You pay extra for your own feed and bedding and must visit the stable at least twice a day to clean the stall, water, feed, groom, and exercise your horse.

A disadvantage here is that you usually have little or no place to store feed and bedding, so you must keep everything at home and lug it back and forth. You end up with your horse practically living out of the trunk or back seat of your car.

Full board includes everything—feed, bedding, cleaning the stall, and sometimes grooming. It starts at about $75 and goes up to $175 or more per month, depending on where you live. The more rural your area, the less expensive the board will be. With full board you have only to do the exercising and pay any blacksmith or veterinary bills.

Services included in the monthly rent vary from stable to stable. Always check to see what yours does include and how much it costs for any extras. Some stables that seem to be cheaper at first will add charges for every little service, so that you are actually paying more. Another factor to consider when choosing a stable is whether or not it has been approved by the SPCA and will give adequate care for your horse.

A stable with turn-out paddocks or fenced-in pastures, where your horse can get out during the day, is preferable to one where your horse has to be cooped up all the time. Turning your horse out will eliminate the necessity of riding every day to keep him exercised. Pastures can also reduce feed bills if they are not overgrazed.

The availability of riding rings and trails is another plus, and an indoor arena might be worth a higher boarding fee if you live in a northern climate with its more severe winters.

An advantage of boarding is that you can usually get a group rate on blacksmith and veterinary bills if all the horses are shod and given their shots at the same time. And if you have full board, you know that your horse will be properly looked after, even if the weather is bad or you are on vacation.

It's a lot easier to find a neighbor to water your plants while the family is away than to find one who will take care of your horse. Some people solve the weather and vacation problem by boarding their backyard horse when they're away and/or for two or three months over the winter, when pitching hay and shoveling manure is most unpleasant.

Another way to save on expenses is to do grooming or cleaning at the stable in exchange for your horse's accommodations. You can also allow your horse to be used by other riders who are taking lessons or hiring a mount for an hour, again for part or all of the board. This will help to keep your pet exercised if you can't ride regularly. The disadvantage of letting your horse be ridden by others is that he may be rented out on weekends and after school when you want to ride.

BACKYARD SUITABILITY

An acre of land is enough for each animal, although the more room your horse has, the happier he will be. Less than an acre—and some horses have considerably less—will be adequate if the horse is given regular daily exercise.

To add to your acreage you could have the barn and a small paddock in your backyard and rent a field from a neighbor.

A check with your local zoning office is in order to see if you have enough land to keep a horse legally on your property. Zoning requirements change as an area becomes more built up. Even though a neighbor has a horse, you may not be able to, if the neighbor acquired his animal before the last zoning change was made.

Your insurance agent can tell you whether additional coverage is necessary. Most companies consider a backyard horse to be like any other pet. If he gets loose and causes damage to your neighbors' property too often and you make claim after claim, the company will probably send out an investigator to see what can be done. His recommendation (putting up a stronger fence in this case) must be followed to avoid stronger measures, such as the raising of your rates or the dropping of your coverage.

A horse that bites or kicks will be compared to a dog that bites. It is recommended that such an animal be sold, for the safety of everyone.

The removal of manure can be quite a problem. Again, there may be rules in your area regarding the amount you may store. One Pennsylvania borough allows horse owners to keep no more than two wagonloads on property within its boundaries—a holdover from the town's horse-and-buggy days. Often, with only one horse, you will be able to distribute all the manure to your neighbors for their gardens and compost piles and still have some for your own use.

Remember to let manure age before putting it around shrubbery, because fresh manure will burn the roots. A good time to work it into your garden is in the fall or winter after harvesting and when everything has died. By the time you are ready to plant in the spring the soil will be well fertilized.

Often, mushroom growers, nurserymen, or farmers are able to use horse manure, although they may not be willing to pick up the manure from only one horse. A last resort is to pay to have it hauled away every month or so.

Is there someone in your neighborhood with whom you can ride? Are there trails and fields to use for riding? Riding alone along heavily traveled

Happiness is looking out your back door in the morning and seeing your own horse waiting for you

roads will eventually become very boring. It's more fun to have a friend to share your horsey interest, to talk to and ride with along trails through woods and meadows.

Neighbors with strong objections to your keeping a horse in your backyard need to be educated and reassured about horses. Tell them about your facilities and safety measures. Often they have had little or no experience with horses outside of a carnival carousel and fear that this monster of yours will knock down fences to attack them on their patios.

Children in the area should also be told about horses and cautioned about the danger of being accidentally stepped on or knocked over. A good practice to enforce right from the beginning is to not allow any children on your property without their parents unless you are there.

To eliminate the everyday drudgery of caring for a horse and still be able to enjoy riding, you might decide to rent a horse for an hour when the mood strikes you or to take weekly riding lessons. But if you want a horse all your own, this is not the most satisfying arrangement. Those who only hire a horse by the hour miss the companionship and fun of knowing and having a horse for a friend.

If, after weighing all the factors involved in keeping a horse in your backyard, you still decide to go ahead with your idea, take things slowly. Don't rush into any purchase or commitment you may later regret. A little common sense used in planning for your new pet will eliminate unnecessary headaches. Don't buy a horse until your facilities—barn and paddock—are ready, or you'll have to spend additional funds on boarding until they are completed.

Remember, your horse should always come first, in spite of personal inconvenience and discomfort. Hearing a nicker as you approach the stall, receiving a ribbon at a local horse show, or being able to daydream on your horse's sunbaked back as he grazes in a field will be well worth the effort and sacrifices you have made for him.

I ♥ HORSES

2
BACKYARD TO BARNYARD

Converting your backyard into a barnyard may be fairly simple, depending on the facilities already there and the area you have available.

A garage or other unused building may need only a few alterations for conversion into a stall. However, if the structure does need a major over-haul, you may find it easier and cheaper to start from scratch and build a new barn in another location.

DRAW A DIAGRAM

Your first step will be to map out your allotted acreage, deciding where your barn, paddock, and manure pile should be placed.

Your local zoning office can tell you if your barn or fence has to be so many feet from a neighbor's property line. The manure pile may also have restrictions on its location, size, and the way it is to be stored, and whether it must be fenced in or covered.

A barn is not an absolute necessity for a horse accustomed to your area's weather, but a shelter of some kind is essential. An unclipped, healthy horse will do fine with a three-sided lean-to that protects him from winter winds and summer sun. The extra expense of an airtight barn with a storage room will make your pet more comfortable, though.

Plan on an area of at least 12 x 20 feet for a one-horse stable and adjoining tack room. A one-stall barn and tack room and a three-stall barn and tack room are shown in the photographs. Remember that the attractive-ness of your barn will be a plus for possible resale later. Water and electricity are luxuries, but they should be close by and convenient to use. A heating system is unnecessary, even in the coldest of climates.

The barn should be close enough to your house for accessibility in bad

A one-horse barn, such as this one with a tack room and paddock, will fit into almost any backyard

weather, but far enough away so that summer flies and smells can't find their way to your patio or indoor living areas. A site approximately 50 yards downwind (in most parts of the country this is to the east) of your home is sufficient. Choose a floor plan and location for your barn that will allow you to add on a stall or two in case you should decide to become a two-or-more-horse family in the future.

The barn door should face toward the south or southeast for extra warmth. Notice from which direction the icy winds of winter sweep across your property. Build the side of your barn that gets hit by the blasts door and window free.

Build your barn inside the paddock or field in a corner or along one side so that the stall door opens out into the fenced area. A horse is happier outside and will leave less of a mess in his stall for you to clean up if he is allowed to roam from stall to paddock as he pleases.

BARN

Your barn should be dry and airy but not drafty, and built on a high, well-drained site. A damp, dark, low stable is a breeding ground for the germs that cause colds, coughs, and rheumatism.

Your horse's stall should have enough room for him to move about freely, and receptacles for feed, water, and rock salt. A tack room or storage area will be a convenience for you and will eliminate hauling your tack, grooming, and cleaning equipment back and forth from your house or garage to the barn.

It is false economy to scrimp on a stall, so plan on a good-sized box —8 x 8 feet for a small pony, 10 x 10 for a large pony, 12 x 12 for a horse —and you will have less cleaning and less wear and tear inside, plus a more contented horse. Since horses can and often do nap while standing, many

This three-stall barn with tack room will accommodate the entire family's horses

people don't realize that if horses have the room, they prefer to lie down to sleep.

A bored, cramped horse, particularly one that is high-strung and nervous, can develop bad habits to relieve nervous energy if he is cooped up in a small stall. You will also appreciate the extra footage if this is the only covered area in which you can groom your horse in bad weather.

A minimum ceiling height of 10 feet and door height of 7 feet are additional safety measures, for they reduce the chances of a rearing horse striking his head.

The stall's door should swing outward or slide to the side and be at least three, but preferably four, feet wide. If a horse becomes ill and lies down next to the door, you won't be able to get in to him if your door swings inward and his body is blocking it. The popular Dutch door is a good choice. The top half can be opened for light and air, while the lower half keeps the horse inside.

Screens for the entire stall door to use during the summer are available for about $40 from most horse equipment stores and catalogs, but old factory window guards costing approximately $10 (if you know of a factory or other abandoned building to be torn down) are just as good. They should be large enough to prevent your horse from going under or over them.

A window opposite the stall door will provide cross ventilation when cool breezes are a premium on hot summer days. The window should swing outward, and if glass panes are used rather than wooden shutters, they should be covered on the inside with heavy screening to prevent your horse from pushing them out and injuring himself on the broken glass.

Frosted glass and dirty panes don't seem to fascinate a horse as much as clean, sparkling windows, so don't bother washing them to allow him to see what's going on outside. He'll only want to poke his nose through the glass.

When choosing the materials to be used in the construction of your barn, you should consider their cost, durability, attractiveness, fire resistance, and maintenance. Cost can range from a few hundred dollars for an inexpensive but adequate facility that you and your family build yourselves to several thousand dollars for a custom-designed showplace.

Some of the materials used in barns are wood (hard woods only, because horses will eat soft woods), including clapboard and plywood with battens; metal; masonry, including concrete, brick, and stone and cinder, concrete, and pumice block; and plastics. Prefabricated barns are also quite popular.

An overhang across the front of your barn is a good place to
crosstie your horse for grooming

The roof should have an overhang of at least three feet in front and back, so rainwater will drain away from the barn. An overhang of six or more feet in front will give you adequate room to crosstie your horse for grooming. The roof should be of wood covered with shingles or metal sheeting and a layer of tar paper on top of the sheeting to muffle the sound of rain or hail.

Your barn's foundation should be deep, to keep water and rodents from getting underneath. Walls should fit tight to the floor so there are no drafts on a horse's feet and legs or back when he is lying down.

Aluminum siding is excellent insulation for walls and will add to the barn's appearance, as will nontoxic paint. A tree or two for shade and shrubbery around the barn's foundation will also enhance its beauty, but they must not be within the horse's reach, because he will chew the bark, eat the leaves, and finally pull the remaining stump right out of the ground.

BARN'S INTERIOR

The floor of the stall will be one of your most important decisions. All materials have definite pros and cons, but several inches of packed clay on top of a gravel foundation for drainage is recommended most often. It cushions a horse's weight and absorbs moisture best. Pawing, however, gouges out holes and gullies that periodically have to be filled in and leveled.

A hard dirt floor is also easy on a horse's legs, but not so absorbent as packed clay, and it also has to be smoothed over when it hollows out.

Wooden floorboards retain moisture and odors, are slippery when wet, and will eventually rot through, with disastrous consequences if your horse's leg slips down between the splintering boards.

Concrete is considered perfectly acceptable by some because it is easy to clean. But it is expensive and very hard on a horse's legs if he is standing in his stall for long periods of time. The same applies to asphalt and blacktop. If you decide on a concrete floor, be sure to rough it up a little so it won't be slippery. Plan on using extra-thick bedding for padding. A gradual slope of one inch every three feet toward the back of the stall to the outside will allow for drainage.

A concrete floor for tack room and storage area, however, is recommended, since it will aid in keeping rodents out of the feed. Another deterrent to rats and mice is a barn cat, which will also provide your horse with some companionship.

Walls between stalls inside the barn should be solid and kickproof, preferably two-by-twelve-inch oak planks. They should be high enough to keep drafts from your horse's back but not so high that he cannot see his neighbor. Heavy wire (not chicken wire) or a slotted partition should be installed from the top of the walls to the ceiling to prevent the horses from reaching over and nipping each other.

The wall between the stall and the feed room should be solid from floor to ceiling so there is absolutely no chance of your horse's ever getting into the grain—a stunt that might cost him his life.

Smooth all wooden edges and try to avoid using any wood that splinters easily in the construction of your barn. Remove all sharp objects that may scratch your horse, countersink all bolts, and keep nails hammered into place.

Trying to save pennies with cheap, poorly made latches, hinges, and other materials may cost you dollars later on in repairs, injuries to your horse, and inconvenience to you.

FEED AND WATER EQUIPMENT

Feed and water equipment should be simple and effective. The equipment may be built in or detached, but removable buckets and tubs are easiest to clean. If you don't have running water in the barn, lay a hose with a shut-off nozzle out to a big tub next to the stable and turn it on and off at your house as you need it.

Water may be provided from an automatic stall waterer or from a pail suspended by a snap hook up on the wall at about the horse's chest height. The pail should be located near the front of the stall for easy refilling. Rubber or plastic pails are better than metal, which tends to have sharp edges when bent or dented.

With many horse owners, hayracks are not so popular as hay nets or just throwing the hay on the floor. In addition to their higher cost, they are even thought to be dangerous. Horses have been known to catch their feet in them or bang their knees up against them. Hay nets, too, have their drawbacks. They can cause eye injuries from dust and small hay stalks.

Grain may be fed in a removable tub, of plastic or rubber, also placed near the front of the stall. It too should be hung at chest height and hold 16 to 20 quarts for horses, 14 to 16 quarts for ponies. Tubs and water buckets each cost under $10.

Another possibility for grain is the extra plastic trash can tops that usually outlast the cans. They can be placed on the floor in a corner—some horse experts argue that eating off the floor is the horse's most natural position anyway. But do not put grain directly on the floor, where worm eggs are more likely to develop in it.

All feeding and watering containers must be wide enough for a horse to put his head down into it, with room to spare all around.

A salt block holder ($2 to $3) should be on the wall next to the water bucket.

Snap hooks on opposite stall walls from each other are a good idea if you have no other covered area to crosstie your horse. Two trees are fine for crosstying him outside, but they're suitable only in good weather.

The tack room and its setup is discussed in Chapter 4 and the food-storage area in Chapter 5.

FIRE SAFETY

Thirty seconds is all you may have to rescue your horse from a burning barn, so put your fire department phone number in a conspicuous spot. Be prepared by having fire alarms, water, and fire equipment available. Know how to use them.

In case of a fire, call the fire department, get your horses out of the barn and tied away from the blaze so they can't run back into what they think is a haven from danger. Then use whatever fire equipment and water you have on hand.

MANURE PILE

The manure pile should be in a secluded spot outside the paddock but within wheelbarrow distance of the barn. It will attract flies, so the farther away from your horse it is, the better. Heaped in a pit or within an enclosed area it is tidier than just dumped on the ground.

PADDOCK

You should have some enclosure in which to turn your horse out so he can move around freely. He should not always be in a stall or staked out in the corner of your yard.

If you have to tie your horse, do so only with the proper equipment —a halter and rope with snap hook. Many horses have never had any experience with ropes and injure themselves in unbelievable ways, so check on yours frequently.

The paddock should be large enough for your horse to be able to take ten running strides. If you're short on space, make the paddock long and narrow rather than square. It should not be used as a grazing area or as a substitute for a pasture.

Level the ground and clear the area of protruding rocks, roots, nettles, weeds, and all plants poisonous to horses, such as yews, autumn crocuses, acorns, and laurel. The trunks of any trees inside the paddock should be wrapped with chicken wire, or your horse may strip off their bark, girdling and killing them. Fruit trees inside the paddock cannot be sprayed with poison, and your horse must be watched so he doesn't gorge himself on green, unripe fruit.

The larger the paddock the less chance there is of its becoming a mudhole. A field used every day by a grazing horse will die off and its soil become soured by his droppings.

Your county agricultural agent or a specialist at your state agricultural college can recommend a specific grass or grass mix and the treatment necessary to help maintain your paddock for a minimal fee. You will need to send him a soil specimen.

If there is no shade available in your paddock, leave the stall door open so your horse can get in out of the sun. Tack curtains made from burlap bags at the top of the door so they hang halfway down over the opening. They will keep the stall's interior cooler and the big horseflies out, while your horse and any breezes can still pass through the door.

FENCES

Good fences keep horses within their boundaries, preventing danger to your equine pets and damage to the neighbors' property.

Recommended materials for horse fences are steel or aluminum posts and rails, wooden posts and rails, wooden posts and boards, and wooden posts and heavy-duty wire.

Wooden posts and rails or posts and boards are the most attractive, but also the most expensive. Wooden posts must be creosoted before being put into the ground to protect them from moisture and eventual rotting.

Save money on posts by using in their place sturdy trees growing along the edge of the paddock. Start your rails and boards two feet up on the posts so that a three-foot fence will be five feet high. Your horse won't crawl underneath it, and the extra height will discourage him from jumping it.

Wooden planks should be fastened to the inside of the posts. This

Horses tend to chew on fences unless you put
a single strand of electric wire across the top

construction is not so attractive from the outside but is much sturdier. If the planks are painted rather than allowed to weather naturally, they will have to be repainted regularly.

Horses tend to chew and lean on fences, so to discourage this practice and preserve your fences add a single strand of electric wire across the top toward the inside of the fence. Any contact with the activated wire will give your horse a jolt—not dangerous—that will remind him to keep his distance. Your neighbors won't like the shock either, so install signs on the fence, warning them of its existence.

If you plan to use only an electric strand to contain your horse, place the wire chest high and teach the animal to respect it. Otherwise, when you turn your pet loose, he may charge through the wire and not even feel the shock. Put a halter and a long lead rope on the horse and allow him to graze up to one of the strands. After touching it at each side of the pasture or paddock, your pet will keep at safe distance.

Wire is the least expensive type of adequate fencing available. Avoid barbed wire, which can do serious injury to a horse if he gets tangled up in it. Instead, use a woven wire fencing with small mesh so your horse can't catch his foot in it. Agricultural wire is cheap but has a weak top and large openings. An electric wire around the pasture or paddock inside the agricultural wire will take care of these shortcomings, however.

Gates should be eight feet wide, solid with sturdy horseproof hardware, either a swinging gate or sliding bars. If sliding bars are used, make sure they are extra long and fit snugly into their holders so your horse can't work them loose.

PLAY EQUIPMENT

Older, docile horses may not need any diversions to keep them occupied, but a young, spirited animal will welcome the chance to play.

A horse loves to roll and scratch his back, especially in the spring when he is shedding his itchy winter coat. A load of sand dumped in a convenient spot in the paddock will be a welcome addition. The sand will be a lot cleaner than mud and manure, and it will even help to groom your horse's coat as you brush it out later.

A plastic gallon milk container hanging from the stall's ceiling at head height can be fun for your horse to poke or butt.

A soccerball or basketball in the paddock can be kicked or pushed from one side to the other. Rearing in mock terror, kicking up heels and charging about at the ball's slightest movement, your horse will use up excess energy on toys rather than vent frustration on your fences and barn walls.

3
PINTO, PAINT, OR PALOMINO?

Buying the right horse requires a great deal of thought before you even start looking. Decide, first of all, your price range, who's going to ride the horse, and what you want to do with him.

WHAT BREED?

Any one of the Light Horse breeds (different from the heavy draft horses used for hauling) are excellent choices, depending on your use. But a purebred—an Arabian, a Morgan, thoroughbred, or quarter horse—is going to be much more expensive than a crossbred or just plain horse, referred to as "grade" or "cold blood."

What you plan on doing with your horse will determine whether you want a horse with some hunter in him for jumping or some quarter horse in his background for gymkhana events such as barrel racing. A quarter horse or a horse with some quarter horse breeding is a good sturdy pet that adapts well to a backyard facility and most demands made by the average rider. A horse with some pony blood usually inherits good sense.

The Heinz 57 variety of horse often exhibits the best of the many breeds in his background and, unless you are planning to show or breed professionally, will do well in your backyard.

A child should not be overmounted, but the horse should be big enough so she won't outgrow him right away

30

WHAT PRICE?

There are no set prices on horses, and their value depends on their age, soundness, conformation, temperament, manners, schooling, breeding, and jumping ability. It is rare for a horse to have all these qualities, so you will have to decide which are most important to you and sacrifice the others.

A good price range for a crossbred or grade horse is between $300 and $700. An unbroken Shetland pony may sell for $10, while purebreds can run into the thousands of dollars. Papered animals, such as thoroughbreds or Arabs, are usually too "hot" or nervous and spirited for a family horse and the novice rider. They are often not so hardy either and will require more exact, specialized care and facilities.

WHAT SIZE?

If the horse is to be ridden only by a small child, then a pony might be the best choice. But if all the family members plan on taking rides now and then, a small horse is the best size. A good average height is between 14.2 and 15.2 hands. (A hand is four inches and is the unit of measurement used in telling horses' and ponies' height. A horse that is 15.2 hands is 62 inches from the ground to the point of the withers.) The dividing line between horses and ponies is 14.2. Under this height, the animal is a pony. Over, it is judged a horse.

If you are a growing teen-ager, do not choose a horse or pony that is just the right size for you now, because in a year you may feel as if your feet are dragging on the ground.

A horse that is much too big is not right either, for you will probably have trouble saddling and bridling him and even brushing his back and head without standing on a box. In addition, more height in a horse usually means more money, too.

A horse is the right size for you when your knees hit the widest part of the horse's barrel as you sit on his back.

WHAT SEX?

The gender of your horse-to-be is another important consideration. Many young people dream wistfully of a fiery, spirited stallion carrying them swiftly over hill and dale, but such a horse is really quite impractical.

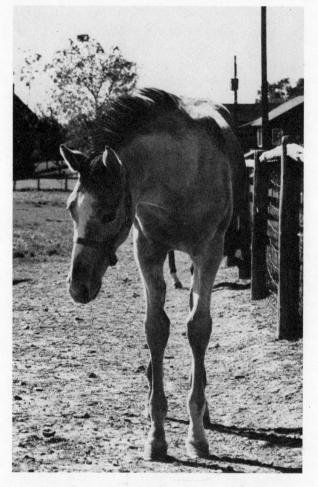

Don't buy a young colt or filly "to grow up with," because it will require experienced handling and professional training

Stallions are usually much too strong for any but the most skilled of equestrians and can be dangerous to riders and other horses if aroused by a mare in heat. Many stables won't even allow stallions to be boarded in their establishments.

Mares are easier to manage than stallions and make good reliable mounts, depending on the individual, except when in heat. Then they may be a little cranky and irritable. A mare will usually come in heat for 4 to 6 days, with intervals between heat periods ranging from 10 to 37 days.

The best choice for a backyard horse is a gelding (a castrated male). Most colts are gelded, so there are many available. They can never be used for breeding, so they are often cheaper than a mare or stallion of equal ability. It is because geldings are most popular for beginners that we usually use the pronoun "he" in this book in talking about your horse.

WHAT AGE?

The age of a horse is not to be overlooked, but for a backyard horse you have quite a wide range of years from which to choose. A horse is said to be in his prime from 3 to 12 years. However, the average riding horse can be between 5 and 18 years. Any horse younger than five will probably be too green and too spirited for the average family. A horse's life-span is between 20 and 30 years, so any animal over 20 is living on borrowed time.

Don't try to predict a horse's soundness by his age. Some horses are old at 10 while others over 25 are still safe, healthy mounts. Not all older horses are necessarily gentle and slow either. Age does tend to mellow most, but it is not an infallible rule.

Older horses tend to be smarter and know all the tricks, but usually they also have more common sense than a younger animal. A horse between 8 and 14 is of a good intermediate age, not too old or too young.

WHAT COLOR?

Color should be the least important of your concerns. Whether your pet is chestnut, roan or bay, pinto, paint, or palomino, as long as he fits your other criteria you should be satisfied. Even though piebalds and skewbalds are generally considered too "loud" for horse shows and English riding, they are fine for gymkhanas and Western riding.

The only real difference in color is that grays, whites, and Appaloosas, which may have higher price tags, are also harder to keep clean, because manure and mud stains show up more and need a little extra scrubbing to remove.

WHAT TEMPERAMENT?

The two most important requirements for a backyard horse are soundness and gentleness—soundness or good health so that you can ride when you want, and gentleness so you do not have to worry that you or neighborhood children will be thrown or kicked.

A spirited horse versus a docile horse is another way of looking at equine temperament, but the ideal animal will really have a little of each. As one father said while out looking for a horse for his daughter, "I want a horse that will give her a good ride without killing her."

A horse with a good disposition and a sensible nature is a joy to work

A too-spirited horse can be dangerous for a young rider

around and ride. Never buy a horse that you fear, because, his behavior will get worse as you become frustrated at your inability to handle him. The horse will sense your fear and try to take advantage of you. The result could be an unnecessary accident.

WHERE TO BUY A HORSE

There are many places to find a horse: through advertisements in your local paper or tack shop, your veterinarian, or word of mouth of horsey friends.

You may even find your ideal pet at the stable where you have been taking riding lessons, although the owner may be reluctant to sell reliable young people's mounts. You might consider asking your instructor what type of horse you should look for to match your riding ability.

Always buy a horse from a reputable, well-recommended dealer. Satisfied customers are the best advertisement, so you can expect fair treatment.

Your veterinarian may know of a family horse for sale. Keep in mind that not all veterinarians treat horses. Some are small-animal practitioners only. Look for those whose specialty is horses, and because of their calls on nearby barns, they will know what's going on with the horsey set in your area.

Caution is advised if you plan to attend the horse auctions that advertise "100 head of fresh horses just in from the West." Horses may seem to be cheaper here than from a private individual, but it takes a real expert and a lot of luck to strike a good bargain. These "Western broomtails" are usually problem horses that no one else in the area wants or those shipped in from another auction. And once you make a winning bid, the horse is yours. There is no trial period or return privilege if you are not satisfied.

Tranquilizing a wild pony or pepping up an exhausted, worn-out horse with hormones is, of course, an illegal practice and hard to detect at crooked auctions, because you have little chance to really examine these animals.

A veterinarian's examination will give you an idea of the animal's general health

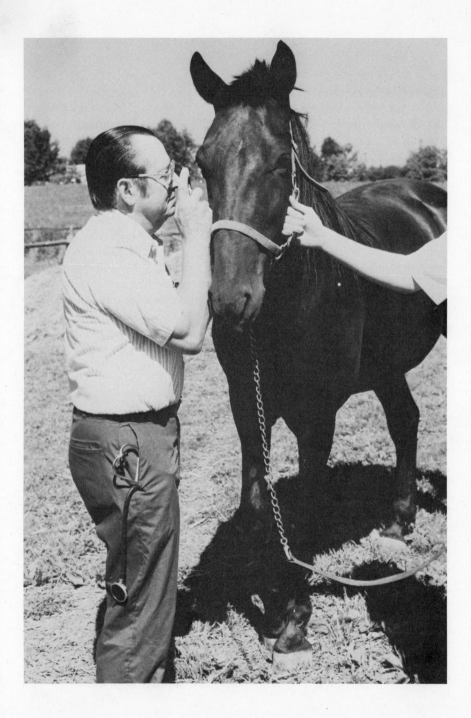

Some sellers have even been known to give shots of novocaine in a horse's legs to eliminate soreness; shoe them in ways to hide poor gaits, sore feet, and lameness; or feed them small quantities of arsenic, which puts almost instant weight on any bag of bones. Without the arsenic (eventually poisonous and addictive), pounds disappear and your newly acquired horse soon returns to his former skeletal condition.

Your local SPCA may also have a horse or a pony for you at a very reasonable price—about $25—if you don't mind taking an animal in poor condition and working to get it back in shape. The SPCA often picks up cruelty cases or receives animals donated by people who cannot afford to keep them any more but want them to get a good home. Before the SPCA will allow you to adopt a horse, it will inspect your facilities, make sure you know how to care for a horse, and check periodically to see that you are keeping the horse in good condition.

Summer camps and seasonal riding academies may offer you a horse for ten months of the year free if you will pay for his feed and board. Another possibility is to care for a horse for a friend or neighbor who is going on a long vacation or going away to college. Riding privileges are yours in return.

HOW TO BUY A HORSE

There are no black-and-white guidelines to follow when buying a horse, so when you are planning to make an actual purchase, be sure to take along a veterinarian and another knowledgeable person to examine the horse. You may be able to see whether a horse is nice-looking or not, but will you be able to tell how old he is and how good his gaits and conformation are? Can you tell whether he is sound and physically able to do what you want—jump, turn quickly, run fast, or participate in fairly long pleasure rides without becoming exhausted?

A veterinarian will charge about $15 to $25 to give you a picture of the horse's general health. The vet will check his age (accurate up to 10 and within 2 to 4 years after that) and try to determine whether the horse will be long-lived.

After carefully checking the horse's eyes, the vet will start at the neck and go all over the body, legs, and feet, looking for faulty conformation that might result in a future disability.

Blood or urine samples can be taken to detect any drugs (not the usual practice with this type of sale), and a Coggins test is done for equine infectious anemia. The veterinarian will also discuss with the owner the horse's medical history and ask what shots and worming have been administered, so that you will know what has to be done as the horse's new owner. He will check the horse's heart and lungs and his wind after he has been ridden.

What a veterinarian cannot do is guarantee a horse completely. A tumor of the internal organs, bone chips, and other problems that may show up only after a period of extensive work or as the horse ages, cannot be spotted.

A veterinarian is not supposed to comment on the horse's training, suitability for the buyer, conformation, and disposition other than what would affect the horse's ability to work. That is what you, the buyer, and your knowledgeable friend must decide.

A trial period of a week or two is given by many sellers, sometimes for an extra fee. If this is impossible, then you should try riding the horse before purchasing to determine his suitability for you. If you are a beginner, let your friend ride the horse for you, trying out all the horse's gaits and testing to see whether he minds traffic and stands for dismounting and mounting.

Approach the horse slowly the first time and let him sniff you, watching for friendly or hostile reactions. Walk all around him carefully to see if he bites or kicks, pick up his feet, and try grooming, saddling, and bridling him to see if you can do it by yourself. Other tests might be to see if the horse can be caught easily in a field and to check on the condition of his stall to see if he kicks the walls, chews, or cribs on the door.

Don't buy the first horse you try. A horse is a long-term investment, so don't buy in haste. Take your time and test several. Anyone selling a reliable, healthy horse should not mind a complete examination. Evaluate the horse's present owner, the care and handling of the horse, and the reason for selling.

Don't always accept the first price. Try to bargain with the seller. Is the horse's tack included or is he to be sold as he stands, with a tattered old halter?

Does he back easily, stand without fidgeting, take both leads when cantering? If Western, does he neck-rein? Do you have to kick him constantly to keep him moving? Does he respond easily to the reins or pull on the bit and take some doing to control? These are all points that you can correct but about which you can haggle to bring the asking price down.

Aim for perfection in your selection and then decide what you can do without. A skinny, unkempt animal with a low price tag may with care develop into a perfectible suitable riding horse for you. A Roman nose is hardly as bad a defect as contracted heels. Perfection costs money, but don't compromise on good manners in and out of the stall, soundness, or gentleness. A horse with quality will also be easier to resell if and when you go on to a more advanced horse.

When you purchase the horse, be sure to receive from the seller a written dated warranty of the terms, the horse's age, soundness in wind and limb, freedom from vices like kicking and biting, and suitability for your purpose. The contract should also state the price, whether tack and transportation are included, whether the seller holds clear title to the horse, and whether the horse can be returned if the above written description is not accurate.

Buying a horse is a personal matter. Be sure to pick one that you like and trust. A feeling of dislike or disinterest is hardly the basis for a partnership of proud owner and willing horse.

4
SNAFFLE TO SADDLE

Tack is the horseman's term for all equipment put on a horse: saddle, bridle, halter, and so on. Before choosing your tack, decide first whether you are going to ride English or Western style. There are different sets of tack, with many variations, for each style. You should not try to mix and match the two kinds of tack, but should acquire either one or the other.

If you have been taking riding lessons, you will probably want to continue in the style that you have been learning. But if you have experience in both English and Western, you will then have to decide what to do with your horse in the future. Speed events, such as barrel races, are much easier to perform with Western gear, but an English hunt saddle is made for jumping. Everyday riding is done with either Western or English tack.

WESTERN TACK

The *Western saddle* was once an intricate part of the Old West. Today's models, often more elaborate than those of the past, are available in three basic frames for: (1) most quarter horses, (2) horses with higher withers, and (3) Arabians.

Western saddles are bought with everything included, but it is a good idea to get a spare girth. Saddles range in price from about $120 for those made in Mexico to several thousand dollars for jewel-encrusted, silver-studded show saddles. The average saddle costs between $300 and $500 (in 1976), although you could find a good American-made saddle for under $300.

A *blanket* or pad should be used under a Western saddle to give added protection to the horse's back. The most popular are the handwoven, wool Navajo blankets that are usually washable. Blankets start at about $10 and

41

go up to almost $30 for one with double fringe. Buy two, especially if you live in a warmer climate, so you will always have a dry one to use.

The *Western bridle,* like its English counterpart, is composed of the bit, the reins, and the headstall. The headstall includes the two cheek straps, a crownpiece, throatlatch, browband and noseband (called a cavesson on the English bridle).

A properly attired Western style rider shows her properly tacked Western style horse

A bosal, which has no bit, is often used for training young horses

There are different bridles for Western pleasure riding, barrel racing, cutting, or training.

A bosal, which has no bit, is often used for training or schooling young horses. It has reins that are knotted under the horse's jaw and a headstall with a plaited rawhide or rope noseband.

The mechanical hackamore, which also has no bit, is hinged to put pressure on the nose and under the jaw. It doesn't give instant and precise control, and is rarely used for reining or pleasure. But it is ideal for barrel racing and roping, where fast starts and sudden stops are needed.

The split-eared type of bridle is the simplest one to put on, is neat, and lately has been the most popular for showing and pleasure riding. Bridles with silver or white buck-stitching are also fashionable and may be teamed up with studs and carvings on wider leather pieces.

Bridles without a bit or reins start at $15.

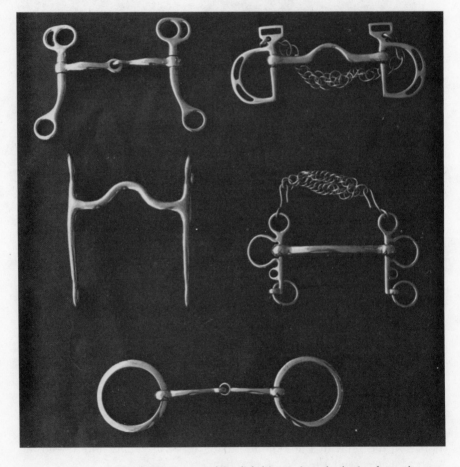

Both Western and English bits, going clockwise from the top right, are: a slotted Kimberwicke, a Tom Thumb Pelham with short shanks, a snaffle, a common Western bit, and a Tom Thumb Western snaffle

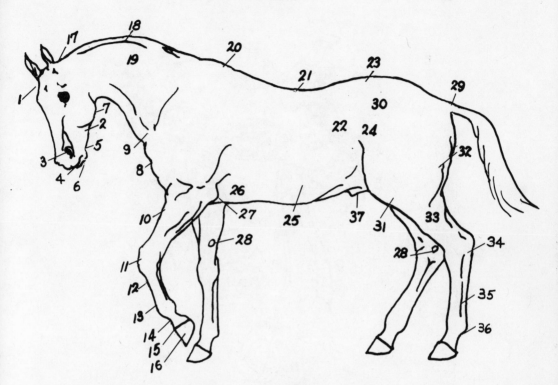

POINTS OF THE HORSE

1 FOREHEAD	20 WITHERS
2 CHEEK	21 BACK
3 NOSTRIL	22 FLANK
4 LIPS	23 CROUP
5 CHIN GROOVE	24 LOINS
6 BARS OF JAW	25 BARREL
7 THROTTLE	26 HEART GIRTH
8 POINT OF SHOULDER	27 ELBOW
9 SHOULDER	28 CHESTNUT
10 FOREARM	29 DOCK
11 KNEE	OR ROOT OF TAIL
12 CANNON	30 POINT OF HIP
13 FETLOCK	31 STIFLE
14 PASTERN	32 POINT OF RUMP
15 CORONET BAND	33 GASKIN
16 HOOF	34 HOCK
17 POLL	35 REAR CANNON
18 CREST	36 REAR FETLOCK
19 NECK	37 SHEATH

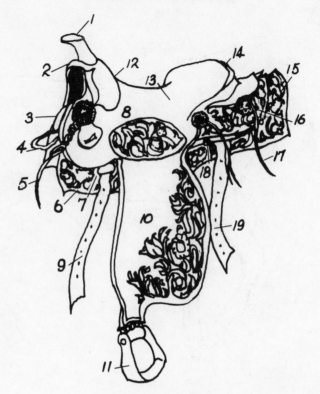

WESTERN SADDLE

1 HORN	11 STIRRUP
2 POMMEL	12 FORK
3 WOOL LINING	13 SEAT
4 ROPE STRAP	14 CANTLE
5 LACE STRING	15 SKIRT
6 SKIRT	16 BACK JOCKEY
7 DEE RING	17 LACE STRINGS
8 FRONT JOCKEY	18 DEE RING
9 FRONT TIE STRAP	19 FLANK GIRTH
10 FENDER	

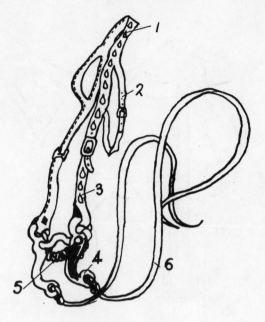

WESTERN BRIDLE

1 SPLIT EAR HEADSTALL
2 THROATLATCH
3 CHEEKPIECE
4 GRAZER BIT
5 CURB CHAIN
6 REINS

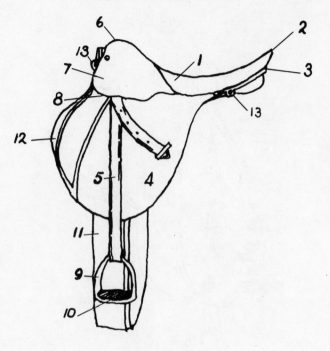

ENGLISH SADDLE

1 SEAT
2 CANTLE
3 PANEL
4 FLAP
5 STIRRUP LEATHER
6 POMMEL
7 SKIRT
8 STIRRUP BAR
9 STIRRUP IRON
10 TREAD
    OF STIRRUP IRON
11 GIRTH
12 KNEE ROLL
13 DEE RINGS

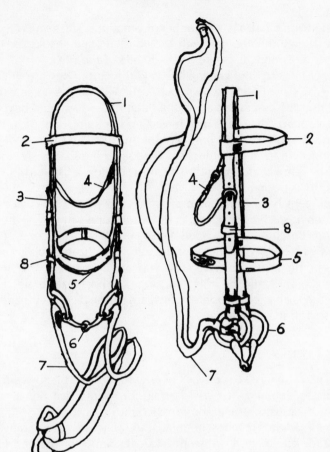

ENGLISH BRIDLE

1 CROWNPIECE
   OR HEADSTALL
2 BROWBAND
3 CHEEKPIECE
4 THROATLATCH
5 CAVESSON
6 SNAFFLE BIT
7 REINS
8 KEEPERS

The *Western bit* also has a number of variations. The gentlest is a shank snaffle—a flexible mouthpiece with a curb chain and shanks for control. However, a bit is only as gentle as the hands of the rider.

Stronger bits are the "grazing bit" and the curb. They are similar, but the grazing bit's shanks curve back out of the way so the horse can graze with the bit in his mouth (an annoying habit that you should never allow your horse to start). They each may have a port or hump on the mouthpiece (the wider and more shallow ports are the mildest), and shanks or cheeks that vary in length from 6 to 9 inches. The longer the shanks are, the more severe the bit is in a horse's mouth. The most severe is a "spade bit"—never to be used by a beginner.

A roping bit has its two shanks curving down and meeting together below the chin, so there is less chance of the rope getting caught in it.

Bits can be chrome- or nickle-plated, copper-coated, or of stainless steel. Stainless steel bits are the most durable. The cheapest bit is about $5.

Reins come in various widths, so you can choose the ones that best fit your hands. They may be of leather, rope, or horsehair, braided or flat. Except for those on a roping bridle, which are of one piece, reins are usually long and split in the middle.

ENGLISH TACK

There are three basic types of *English saddles:* the forward seat or hunt saddle for jumping, the park saddle for saddle seat riding, and the all-purpose style for dressage and cross-country riding.

The hunt saddle is the most popular among English riders. It ranges from about $70 for one made in Argentina to over $500 for the best German model. The average hunt saddle costs from $150 to $300.

Unlike Western fittings, stirrups (leathers and irons) and girth usually do not come with the English saddle. You must buy them separately.

Stirrups are either nickle- or chrome-plated, or of stainless steel. They may have rubber treads. The "never-rust" ones are the most practical, and stainless steel the hardest. Make sure the stirrup fits your foot. The widest part of your foot should fit into it with an inch to spare on each side.

Also available are safety stirrups and offset stirrups. Safety stirrups have a heavy rubber band on one side of the stirrups so that if you fall and your foot is caught, the band will unhook, releasing your foot. Safety stirrups should always be used on bareback pads where stirrups are attached to metal dees rather than a saddle's safety bar. Offset stirrups have the slot for the leather off center (to the right on a right-hand iron). This throws the knee in, and the sloping footrest keeps the heel down. Some people feel that this stirrup helps their position during a show.

Stirrups range from $6 to $36, depending on their size and quality.

Leathers range in price from $5 for a children's size to $15–$25 for those made in England of top-quality leather.

Girths are available in leather, vinyl, webbing, cord, mohair, or nylon. They may also be shaped at the horse's elbows to prevent chafing. The cord and mohair girths are washable. They allow air to circulate through them, and so are practical for a very hot day or on muddy trails. Have two—a mohair one and another of leather for everyday use and showing.

Girths cost from under $10 to over $40.

Pads under English saddles help to protect both the horse's back and the underside of the saddle. (A horse's sweat can rot the leather.) These pads are made of synthetic sheepskin or Equi-Fleece, which is mothproof and mildewproof and can be thrown into the washer, real sheepskin, felt, quilted flannel, and wool. Double-faced pads are available for supersensitive backs.

English riders do not usually use a pad in a show because it does not give a neat appearance. However, they do give their saddles an extra scrubbing afterward.

Pads start at $7 and go up to $38 for a genuine sheepskin pad. The average cost is around $15.

English bridles and *bits,* and what combination to buy, depend on what the horse is being used for and the education of both horse and rider. There are show bridles, Pelham bridles, snaffle bridles, Weymouth bridles, and walking horse bridles that come with or without bits and reins.

Bits range from the gentle snaffle and the soft rubber-mouth Pelham to the Kimberwicke and the more severe high port brace cheek walking bit. There are additional variations among the bits, and some come with a curb chain. Try the gentlest possible bit first and work up to stronger ones, until you find the right combination for controllability.

Borrow some bits from friends. Try them to see which one your horse accepts and works best with before you buy.

Reins can be all leather (braided, laced, rubber-coated, or plain), of linen cord, or of strong webbing. They also come in various widths (¼ inch to 1 inch) to fit your hand.

English bridles start at under $15 and may go up to over $100. The average one costs between $20 and $40. Bits start at a couple of dollars and go up in price to over $30. Reins start at about $5, but may cost more than $35 if you choose raised braided ones.

TACK ACCESSORIES

There are a number of other pieces of equipment that you will need, but do not buy everything that catches your eye. Many inexperienced horse owners go overboard and never use half of what they buy. The more equipment you put on your horse (running martingales, fancy bits, etc.), the more "crutches" you are using in order to ride him. A lightweight bridle and simple snaffle suffice for a competent rider and a well-mannered horse.

Although a breastplate, martingale, saddlebags, and spurs may appeal to you, they may not really be necessary. Breastplates are for horses with heavy or undefined withers to keep their saddle in place during a strenuous ride or when making quick turns.

Martingales or tie-downs (Western) keep a horse's head down. Be sure the one you use is not too tight, and does not hinder your horse's balance.

Saddlebags and spurs are useful items, too, but if you have no use for the bags and your horse has no need of the spurs, they are a waste of money. Remove your spurs when you are working on the ground so they don't trip you.

A crop, bat, whip, or quirt (whatever name you prefer) should be used with discretion, and should rarely be in the hands of a beginner.

Halters and *lead ropes* are essential pieces of tack to be included in your barn. Depending on your horse, the climate you live in, and how your horse will be used, you may also want to add a longeing rein, blankets, and a sheet or cooler to your shopping list.

Halters are made of leather, nylon, or braided cotton. Leather and nylon halters are most popular, and each has its pros and cons. Leather will break if yanked hard enough (which some horsemen feel is a plus in certain emergencies, such as when a horse catches his hoof in it). If wide enough, leather is also less likely to chafe the skin.

Nylon halters are less expensive and last longer, but they won't break and are more apt to rub and even cut your horse. Halters cost about $5 for nylon ones to $10 and up for those of leather. Have at least two, one as a spare for the times the other is mislaid.

FITTING YOUR TACK

The most important point to remember when buying your horse's tack is that it should fit him without the use of any homemade devices such as extra blankets or pads to keep the saddle's pommel from pressing into his withers or spine.

There are adjustable headstalls for large and small heads, bits in various sizes (4½ inches for ponies to 5½ inches for horses), and saddles with cut-back pommels for horses with high withers.

Unlike the other pieces of tack, the saddle should fit the rider as well as the horse. Hunt saddles come in several sizes, from 15 inches for children to 19 inches for adults. Equitation (flat) saddles go up to 21 inches, and Western saddles have seat sizes of 13, 14, 15, and 16 inches. Your tack shop owner should be able to measure and fit you for a saddle.

BUYING TACK

Tack is available in various qualities. The cheaper pieces of gear may be bought for less money initially, but in time you may have to spend money on repairs and replacements. You must also take better care of cheaper tack to maintain it.

The most expensive tack is for those who can afford the very best in leather, craftsmanship, and sometimes the snob appeal of sporting the brand name of a well-known European saddlemaker.

Buy the best quality of medium-priced tack that you can afford from a reputable firm. With proper care, your equipment will last for many years.

If you cannot afford to buy a new quality saddle (your most expensive item), check a reliable tack shop for trade-ins. They may have just what you want at a more reasonable price and already broken in. Be sure the tree is sound and the stitching intact.

Used tack is also a good idea for someone with a first horse who has not completely decided on a riding style and may switch from English to Western, or vice versa.

CLEANING TACK

Many horse owners take great pride in cleaning their tack. More important is the fact that clean, regularly checked bridles, reins, stirrup leathers, and girths may actually save you from a nasty fall. A new saddle should be oiled before it is used.

Ideally, your tack should be wiped off after each use. However, once a week is sufficient. The longer you wait to clean it, the dirtier and more time-consuming the job will be. Left dirty too long, the leather may dry out, eventually having to be replaced.

To clean your tack you will need:

glycerin or saddle soap	a chamois cloth
neat's-foot oil or Lexol	flannel rags
metal polish	towel scraps
a stiff brush	an old toothbrush or nailbrush
a Tuffy	wooden matches or toothpicks
a small natural sponge (not to be used on your horse)	

Start with the saddle. If there is any mud on it, let it dry and then brush it off with the stiff brush.

Remove all the saddle's fittings and take the bridle apart. Remember how everything fits together—what attaches to what—so you can put it back together again after it has been cleaned. Soak stirrup irons, curb chain, and bit in warm soapy water. Then, using a Tuffy and a toothbrush, scrub the dirt buildup from corners and crevices. Do not use steel wool on the bit, because it will leave flakes of iron on the mouthpiece. Wash the stirrups' rubber treads and put them aside to dry.

Soak the girth, if it is washable, and the pads in cool water and mild soap. Later, machine-wash them in cold water, using a mild soap. Dirty, crusty pads can cause sores, but a strong detergent may also irritate the horse's skin. A leather girth should be cleaned with the saddle.

Wash the underside of an English saddle (a Western saddle is lined with real or imitation sheepskin) and leather girth with lukewarm water, mild soap, and rough towel scraps, scrubbing hard to remove all the sweat, dirt, and accumulated hair. It is important not to get leather too wet, so dry it immediately with a chamois cloth.

Then, using the sponge and as little water as possible, apply saddle soap to all leather except an English saddle's suede knee rolls, which can be brushed. Rub the saddle soap in and let it dry.

Repeat these same steps with the bridle and fittings, making sure to wash away the buildup of sweat from the inside of the headstall before applying the saddle soap. Saddle soap is not just a cleaner, but is a protective, waxlike covering for leather pieces.

While the leather pieces are hanging up to dry, use the wooden matches or toothpicks to push the soap and dirt out of the buckle holes.

Polish all metal pieces and shine them with clean pieces of flannel. A light coat of petroleum jelly on the bit will keep it from pitting or rusting.

Using a towel scrap, wipe Lexol or neat's-foot oil into the underside of the saddle's flaps and fenders and into any dry leather except the saddle's seat and outside flaps, where it would come off on your clothing. This step is not necessary every time you clean your tack. Leather will wear and crack without lubrication, but don't overdo it. Too much oil may eventually rot the stitching.

When you have finished scrubbing, brushing, oiling, and shining, put everything back together. Tack must be cleaned regularly to keep it soft and pliable.

Do not leave your tack outside if the temperature drops below freezing.

JODHPURS OR JEANS

Around the barn and out on the trails, casual jeans and boots or hard shoes are most practical.

Rubber riding boots are best for mucking out stalls, sloshing around in spring's inevitable mud, and plowing through winter's snowdrifts. They are not designed to keep your feet warm, so room for an extra pair of thermal socks during winter months will be necessary.

The hard hunt caps are a must while jumping, and for safety's sake they should be worn whenever you are riding. Girls over eighteen wear hunt derbies in horse shows.

WESTERN CLOTHING

Western clothing for a horse show includes boots, a felt or straw hat, pants that have a little flare to go over the boots, and a Western shirt or turtleneck bodysuit. Some participants wear knitted, pullover vests or a Western jacket and tie. For American Horse Shows Association (AHSA) events, a poncho should be tied to your saddle, and, except for equitation classes, chaps should be worn.

If you have good posture, a bodysuit will highlight it. Questionable posture can be camouflaged by a shirt. Be critical and see what you look best in—color and style—before you buy.

ENGLISH CLOTHING

For an English equitation or hunt class you should wear short jodhpur boots with jodhpurs, or breeches with high boots and your coat and hunt cap. (The rule of thumb is: jodhpurs when you are mounted on a pony, breeches when you are riding a horse.) You may wear a ratcatcher shirt, with choker and stock pin, a white shirt and necktie, or a turtleneck. Gloves are optional, but desirable.

Visit a local horse show and see what most of the riders in your area are wearing. Then buy moderately priced clothes. A black jacket is more flattering for a heavy person than plaids or checks.

Tightly rolled newspapers or magazines put in your boots when they are not being used will help to keep their shape without the expense of boot trees.

TACK ROOM SETUP

The ideal tack room is one built into your barn, but it can be a back porch, a spare closet, or the corner of a garage. It doesn't have to be elaborate or expensive, just convenient and well organized.

The saddle can be stored on a foldaway steel saddle rack or on a two-by-four wrapped with old pads or feed sacks to protect the leather. It should allow air to circulate underneath for drying. The English saddle should be stored with its stirrup irons run up and its girth unbuckled and laid flat across the saddle, with its ends through the irons. Your saddle pad should be laid on top upside down so it can dry, too.

Bridles should not be hung over a single nail, since the sharp bend there can eventually damage the leather. A wooden half-moon, 6 inches across and 1½ inches wide attached to the wall curved side up, is perfect for hanging up the bridle. Loop the reins over the top of it. Wide shallow tin cans, such as those that contain tuna fish, are also ideal bridle holders. Cover one with adhesive shelf paper to improve its looks before nailing it to the wall.

Heavy pegboard on one wall, with a variety of hooks, will come in handy for those extra bits, straps, and ropes. Brushes, combs, picks, rags, and other grooming equipment that you will accumulate can be stored on shelves.

For all medicines, ointments, and other first-aid items, an old medicine or kitchen cabinet that can be closed should be placed high up on another wall away from little fingers.

Blankets, extra tack, buckets, pans, and pads can be stored in a second-hand trunk. A blanket rack across the back of the door can be easily and inexpensively made out of a heavy-duty towel rack or two half-inch pegs with a nylon rope strung between them.

A bridle can be draped over a two- or four-pronged hook for cleaning

Clean the saddle on a sawhorse or other movable rack right in the tack room. For cleaning, bridles can be draped over a two- or four-pronged hook hanging down from the ceiling.

Grain cans can also be stored in the tack room. A secure door with a latch is a necessary precaution if the tack room is located within reach of your horse. A curious horse can cause considerable damage to both himself and your tack by nibbling on leather pieces or prying open the feed bins.

Ingenuity, throwaways, and scraps are all that are needed to transform your corner of piled-up tack and equipment into a neatly organized tack room.

5
ROOM AND BOARD FOR HORSES

Horses should be fed according to individual needs. These needs will depend on many things: age and size, health and temperament, the kind and degree of activity, the climate and the season of the year.

A horse should be fed with a goal of longtime service rather than temporary economy. Ask your vet to help you set up your horse's feeding schedule. If your horse is in good condition, you might ask the former owner what he has been using for feed. Never depend on the instructions on a bag of feed—they have been written by a promoter trying to sell more of a company's products.

WHEN TO FEED YOUR HORSE

As important as what to feed your horse is when to feed him. A horse is a large animal, needing a great deal of food but with a stomach too small to handle the entire daily nourishment at one time.

A horse is a grazing animal and prefers to eat small amounts of food several times a day. Too much of anything, whether it is the right or the wrong food, may cause stomach problems, such as colic (see Chapter 9).

Some guidelines to remember when feeding your horse:

1. Give several small feedings rather than one large feeding.

2. Feed according to how hard the animal is being worked.

3. Avoid sudden changes in the feeding schedule, and in the kind and amount of food offered.

4. Water the horse first before feeding him.

5. Never feed or water the horse until he is sufficiently cooled off after a workout.

6. Never ride the horse immediately after feeding him.

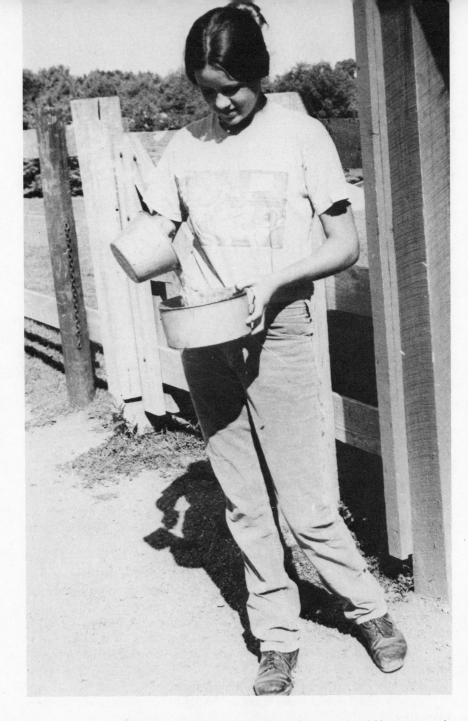

Grains are high-energy foods, and rations should be measured carefully so they are the same at every feeding

Your horse should be fed at least twice a day. Divide the daily ration by the number of times you plan to feed. You might give half the grain and hay in the early morning, the other half of the grain in late afternoon, and the rest of the hay before going to bed so your horse has something to nibble on during the night. It's a good pacifier.

Once you have set up your feeding schedule, stick to it. A horse is a creature of habits, so avoid changing the routine. He will be unhappy if his regularly scheduled mealtime is delayed. Feed in this order: water, hay, and then grain—and only what your pet will clean up without hesitation. A horse with water in his stall will drink the proper amount without supervision from you.

Seasonal adjustments should be gradual—less grain if there is an opportunity to get nourishment from fresh grass in the spring and early summer. But a horse that will suddenly be standing idle for even a couple of days after a routine of hard work should have the grain feeding cut down immediately by a half or even a full quart.

Grains are high-energy foods and if you continue to feed the usual amount without the usual work, your horse may get sick, and even suffer azoturia (see Chapter 9). At the very least, your pet will have an overabundance of energy, possibly too much for you to control.

Any subtractions from or additions to your horse's diet should be gradual. Be careful when changing from one grain to another. Some grains weigh more, and others take up more space. It may require some figuring to come up with the same portions. Institutional-size fruit and vegetable cans and two-pound coffee cans are convenient measuring containers.

You want to water your horse before giving grain, because the water may wash the food right through the system too fast for the body to retain any of the nutrition. Grain has a tendency to swell when wet, so a horse watered after a grain feeding may develop a bad case of colic.

Once you have established what and how much you will feed, keep an eye on your pet's condition to see if he is gaining or losing weight. More backyard horses are too fat rather than too thin, because they aren't being exercised regularly.

A horse that is fed too much hay will develop a hay belly. Those that are not fed enough will become thin, with hollow flanks, and require many months of good feeding to cover their ribs again.

If a horse has a tendency to have leg or foot problems, don't put any extra weight on him.

Before putting your too heavy horse on a diet, check with your vet for an opinion. Your horse may look fat to you, but it might just be the type of build. A chunky quarter horse may appear overweight next to a lanky thoroughbred or vice versa, but actually they may both be just right.

WHAT TO FEED

Feed is the horse owner's greatest single expense, but costs can be kept down through careful, conscientious feeding rather than through nutrition-depriving shortcuts. Your horse will get out of his food only what is there, so spend a little more for quality. It will be worthwhile. A healthy horse, free of internal parasites, is less expensive to feed than a sickly animal that you are constantly nursing back to health.

Complicated mixtures of expensive rations are not necessary. Most horses will do very well on water, hay, oats, some corn supplemented with salt, and a simple combination of minerals.

Water is essential to good nutrition. It should be fresh, clean, and available to your horse at all times unless he is overheated. A mature horse will normally drink 8 to 10 gallons of water a day, and more on a hot day or after a good workout. Don't rush an animal when he is drinking.

A moving stream or stream-fed pond is best for the pasture, but a watering trough is all right, too, if it is periodically scrubbed clean of all encrusted dirt. A small strainer hung nearby is ideal for skimming leaves and grass off the top of the water. All water buckets should be washed out every week so they do not spread diseases.

Snow is too cold to substitute for water in the winter, so break the ice in your horse's water bucket or trough so he can drink whenever he wants to.

Grass is the natural food of horses. However, hardworking animals need supplemental energy foods, such as oats or a grain mixture, to keep them fit.

The nutritional value of a pasture depends upon the amount, the maturity, and the type of forage available. As the green grass of spring matures, it increases in fiber and decreases in nutritional value. The dry brown grass of fall and winter is usually low in protein and vitamins, so you will have to give your horse other feeds during those seasons.

Grass is the natural food of horses

A good pasture helps to lower feed costs if enough acreage is available and if it is kept free of parasites. A one- or two-acre pasture will provide a horse with 3 to 6 months' grazing, depending on the weather. Since lethal sprays are used in many areas, be sure your pasture has not been contaminated by chemicals that have drifted from a nearby orchard. For this same reason you should not allow your horse to nibble the grass along a roadside. Mow your pasture twice a year to keep the weeds under control.

When spring comes and bright green sprouts shoot up all over your horse's field, don't let him out to graze all day right away. Introduce him slowly—an increase of thirty minutes every day—until his body can adjust to the extra richness of new grass.

Hay is the single food most consumed by backyard horses. Legume hays, such as alfalfa and clover, are higher in protein, carotene, and minerals than grass hays, such as timothy or blue grass. They are also more expensive and, if given alone, too rich. They are most often mixed with a grass hay (clover with timothy is a popular mix) for the average riding horse. Some farmers plant clover and timothy together in their fields, so that when harvested the hay is already mixed.

Good hay is never cheap, but buy the best you can afford and you may be able to save on grain. Once you have found a good source of quality hay at a reasonable price, don't lose it. They're tougher to find than the proverbial "needle in the haystack."

Bales of hay vary in weight, but all are tied with either string or wire. Once opened, the bale will fall into sections or "flakes." You can always keep track of how much you feed your horse by how many sections you give him daily.

Whether the hay is a legume or a grass, it should be a faded green in color and free of any mold or excessive dustiness. Early cut hays with a high proportion of leaves to stems is generally higher in nutrition than a stemmy, coarse hay cut in the mature stage. Hay should be properly cured and dried. Moldy hay is poisonous and can kill your horse.

Open one or two bales to examine the hay before paying for an order. If the farmer won't allow this, buy a bale or two, open them to see if the hay is fresh and green, not dry, crumbled, and dusty. If you are satisfied, then give your order.

Grains include oats, corn, barley, wheat, and bran. They are high-energy foods for horses. Ponies don't usually require any grain unless heavily worked and then only a handful or two are necessary.

Grain should be clean and bright-colored, and oats plump and full with

Hay is the single food most consumed by backyard horses

a sweet smell. A dull gray color indicates musty or moldy oats.

Oats are available whole, crimped, or crushed. Whole oats are not so dusty as the other two and you can see what you are getting, but many horses don't chew them properly. Crimped oats with barley and molasses are good for fussy eaters.

Corn is a good addition to your horse's diet in the winter because it helps to produce body heat. However, do not give any corn if your horse is prone to colic.

Corn on the cob is an excellent diversion for nervous or cooped-up horses. Give two large ears of corn at night for your horse to munch on.

Bran acts as a laxative and should be given only in small amounts to your horse. A handful mixed in with your horse's daily ration as a dietary supplement is sufficient. If your horse's droppings are too runny, cut back on the bran or meal, and if they're too hard, give more.

Hot bran mashes consist of bran, oats or a mixed feed, salt, molasses, and boiling water for steaming. They are said to be as healing as "mother's chicken soup" and should be served warm.

Soybean, linseed, and cottonseed meal are protein supplements. They contribute to a glossy coat and are good for the bowels. Add a handful of one to the grain ration three times a week.

Ready-mixed or sweet feeds are usually easier to store and less time-consuming for the single horse owner to prepare than keeping on hand all the different grains. They are also more expensive, but do provide a well-rounded diet with a combination of grains, salt, fish meal, linseed, assorted trace minerals, and, if a sweet feed, molasses.

Pelleted feeds for horses have become very popular in recent years. They are made from several different combinations of grain and hay, and take the place of both. Their advantages include: a more balanced ration; less waste; no dust to irritate horses with respiratory diseases such as the heaves (see Chapter 9); less bulk to ship, handle, and store; and no lost leaves as happens when such hays as clover and alfalfa are mashed together.

The cost of pellets is the biggest disadvantage. However, this may be offset by the high price a single horse owner may have to pay for a few bales of hay because he has very little storage space.

Pellets also contribute to wood-chewing in horses that are confined. This nervous habit can be reduced, however, by including some hay—necessary for roughage—with the daily ration of pellets to give the horse something else to chew.

Salt blocks should also be available for your horse to lick. They can be bought at your local feed store or tack shop. Salt helps the body to retain water and is especially important in the summer when the heat makes a horse sweat a great deal. Place a large block in your pasture under a shelter so the rain won't erode it, and a smaller one in your horse's stall. On the average, a horse will need about one pound of salt a week. Use iodized salt in iodine-deficient areas.

The equipment for feeding and watering your backyard horse has

*Horses need clean bedding and their stalls cleaned every day
if they are kept inside*

already been discussed. There are several options, all with pros and cons (see Chapter 2).

PROBLEM EATERS

A horse that bolts his feed should be discouraged from continuing this habit. To do this, use a special feeding dish or place a tennis-ball-sized rock in his dish to slow him down. You can also give him his hay first to take the edge off his appetite.

Finding whole grains of corn and oats in the manure is a good indication of bolting. A horse with this habit does not get the full value of his food.

Picky eaters need some chopped-up carrots and a little molasses, sugar, or honey added to their grain to entice them to clean their feed bins. Other vegetables, such as turnips and sugar beets, and fruits, such as peaches, apples, and pears, will also encourage them to eat. Be sure to cut up the fruit, removing all pits. Do not overfeed these tantalizers. No more than two apples a day.

BEDDING

Horses confined in a stall need good clean bedding daily because, although they do a lot of napping standing up, they also like to lie down to rest.

There are several things that you can use to bed your horse down. They all have their advantages and disadvantages, which may differ according to what part of the country you live in and what is available.

Straw, peat moss, wood shavings and sawdust, and shredded sugar-cane are the more commonly used materials.

Straw provides good drainage, dries fastest, and looks clean and fresh. However, some horses may try to eat it, and, being bulky, it creates bigger manure piles, and needs more room for storage.

Wood shavings and sawdust are available at no cost in some areas, but you will have to bag and transport them back to your barn. They are dusty, not very absorbent, and mat down quickly, so you have to use more for a soft bed. Sawdust and mud can make quite a mess in a long tail, so a mud knot (see Chapter 8) is a good idea.

Peat moss is expensive, but after it has been used in the stall and aged, it is all ready to use in gardens and around bushes as a mulch-fertilizer.

Never buy moldy hay for bedding, because your horse will eat it and stand a good chance of being poisoned.

STORAGE

A storage area for hay and bedding can be on the second floor of your barn, in a room next to the stall or even in a separate building. It should be kept dry so that it doesn't become moldy. Air should be allowed to circulate under the bales to lessen the chance of spontaneous combustion and fire. Provide for this by piling the bales onto a wooden platform or framework of thick boards a few inches from the floor. Never stack them too close to a light bulb, though. The heat from the bulb may start a fire, too. A wire shield several inches in diameter around each bulb will keep you from accidentally stacking the hay too close to them.

To eliminate constant trips to a farmer or dealer for more hay, you will need a large storage area. It will also be cheaper as well as more convenient if you can buy a year's supply at one time—about one ton for one horse. Buy your supply in summer or early fall to get the lowest price. Share the cost and divide an order of hay and/or grain with a friend or two if you have limited space for storage or think the food will be too old by the time your horse gets to the "bottom of the barrel."

Some feed dealers will deliver your order free of charge if you buy a minimum number of pounds of grain or bales or tons of hay.

Grains should be stored in closed containers, such as garbage cans (galvanized metal is sturdier than plastic) with tight-fitting tops. Be sure that all the grain is used up in the can before you dump a fresh bag in. The bottom grain can make your horse very sick if you hold it over until the end of another order.

6
GROOMING STEED AND STALL

Caring for a horse is time-consuming and just plain hard work. Keeping your horse in good condition—healthy and well groomed—should be satisfying work, though, especially when you know that your pet is fit enough to enjoy a ride as much as you.

As a horse owner you will spend many more hours brushing, picking, washing, clipping, shoveling, sweeping, and feeding than riding. However, this is the time that you will also have a chance to really get to know your horse's habits, quirks, likes and dislikes.

STABLE EQUIPMENT

In order to care for your horse properly you will need special equipment and plenty of elbow grease.

FOR GROOMING YOU WILL NEED:

a rubber currycomb

a stiff dandy brush

a soft dandy brush or body brush

a large plastic comb for mane and
tail

clean towels

a sweat scraper

a shedding blade

a bucket

shampoo

coat conditioner

3 sponges (2 small, 1 large)

fly repellent

a hoof-pick

hoof dressing

body clippers (optional)

70

FOR STALL CLEANING:

a manure fork

a pitch fork

a flat-ended shovel

a heavy-duty push broom

a standard house broom

a rake

a wheelbarrow or manure basket

hydrated lime or liquid
    disinfectant

OTHER EQUIPMENT:

wire clippers

a hammer

pliers

a screwdriver

a leather punch

a garbage can for trash

a fire extinguisher

These items can be bought at a tack shop, hardware store, or feed store.

GETTING TO KNOW YOUR HORSE

The day your new horse arrives and takes his place in your back-yard will be one of ecstasy and joy for you, but confusing and possibly frightening to the horse. The animal will need time to get used to new surroundings. Love and attention from you will help.

When you approach a strange horse, do it slowly and cautiously, but confidently. Try not to be nervous or afraid, because a horse can sense your feelings and may react accordingly—either fearfully, too, or bullying.

Let the horse sniff your hand. Then pet him firmly on the neck or shoulder—never a timid stroke on the nose. Most horses hate that.

It will be up to you to reassure and welcome your horse to his new home. Start by letting him become accustomed to you. Always move slowly and never dart or sneak around him. Give plenty of warning of your next action—a pat on the rump as you walk behind him, a few words as you pass by carrying a saddle, bridle, or other miscellaneous equipment. Startling the animal could prompt a kick.

Spend as much time as you can being with your horse, working around him, and introducing him to the barn, paddock, or pasture, the tack, and especially to you. Sit outside the stall and do your homework, read a book

Caring for a horse is time-consuming, and grooming requires plenty of elbow grease

nearby while the animal grazes, or just stand at the door and talk. Continuous chattering is pleasing to a horse and even a radio's rock music and DJ's nonsense is soothing.

A new horse will usually be too excited in an unfamiliar stall to lie down at night, but this is natural. It may take a few days before your pet relaxes enough to take advantage of that fresh, soft bed you have slaved over.

If you have another horse, do not turn them out together until they get to know each other. Instead, ride them side by side in the ring or out on the trail. Turn them out in adjoining paddocks so they can meet each other over the fence. When you do eventually put them in the same field, watch for any signs of trouble.

There will probably be some initial squealing and kicking up of heels, but this is to be expected until the "pecking order" is established. The pecking order is a social system that establishes which animal is the leader, which is second in line, and so on down to the last horse, who knuckles under to all the others. The most aggressive and cleverest horse, rather than the biggest and strongest, usually ends up as the Big Cheese.

If you can, remove your horses' hind shoes before turning them out together. Horses without shoes will do less damage to each other if a kick does connect during this testing period.

GROOMING

Grooming is an important part of horsekeeping and should be done before and after every ride. It stimulates circulation, contributes to good muscle tone, and puts the sheen in a horse's coat.

Even a horse that is not ridden should be groomed every couple of days. Accumulated dirt on a horse left out for the winter acts as an insulator against cold winds and freezing temperatures, but an occasional brushing will keep his coat in better condition. It also gives you a chance to check for cuts and other injuries.

The most convenient way to groom a horse is to put him in crossties. The ideal place is in a hallway or covered area outside the stall, but if you do not have such a spot, then crosstie him in his stall or, in nice weather, between two trees.

Wear an apron or a smock to protect your good clothing, and a scarf to keep your hair clean. Otherwise, wear old clothes.

There are numerous ways in various sequences to groom a horse. The logical place to start is at the top. Work down and from front to back. Never

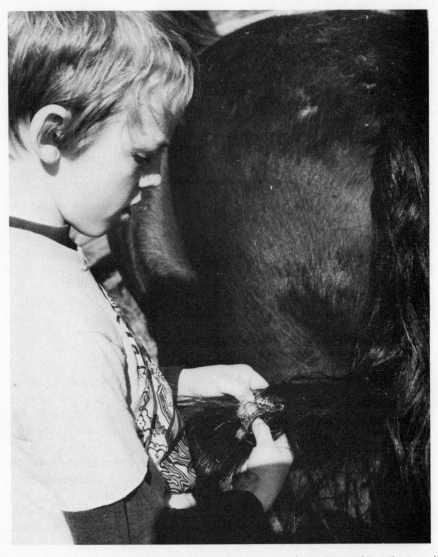

Never stand directly behind your horse. Bring his tail around to you when pulling out a burr

stand directly behind your horse. Pull the tail around to where you are standing to brush it.

1. Using the rubber currycomb at the top of the neck on the near or left side, rub it in a circular motion against the hair. Do this all over the horse's body to remove dried mud and caked-on sweat. Be careful of your horse's sensitive flanks and girth area. Do not use the currycomb on your horse's face or below his knees and hocks.

Knock the dirt and old hair out of the comb by banging it face down on a hard surface, such as a wall, post, or door. Later brush the marks off with a broom.

2. The stiff dandy brush should be used next to brush away the dirt loosened by the currycomb and to clean the legs from the knees and hocks down. Brush with the hair in short strokes. Also brush out the mane and tail. Do not use it on the horse's face.

Clean the brush frequently by rubbing it against the currycomb.

3. Use the soft dandy brush or body brush on the horse's face and ears, shielding his eyes one at a time with your other hand to prevent dust from blowing into them.

Clean the soft brush against the stiff one as you work.

4. Then wipe the horse with a clean towel to give the coat an extra glow.

5. Start with the left front foot and clean the horse's feet with a hoof-pick. Facing the horse's tail, hold the hoof with your left hand and support it on your left knee. Pick away from you along each side of the frog to remove any packed mud, manure, or bedding.

Clean the left hind foot next, then the right front and right rear ones.

6. Take a small damp sponge and wipe away any secretions from eyes and nostrils.

7. The dock and udder area should also be wiped off daily with a second damp sponge, and the sheath of a gelding should be washed about every two weeks with warm water and a mild soap. Do not interchange your sponges.

8. During the fly season, spray or wipe on fly repellent. Never spray around the horse's face.

A thorough grooming as described above should always be given your horse before you go for a ride. However, if your horse is cooled off after you have ridden, you need only give him a light brushing then. A damp body sponge is good for removing the sweat and salt that have accumulated under and around the saddle, girth, and bridle. Sponging also seems to speed up the drying process.

Lead the horse around to dry after sponging. Do not turn him out, for he will roll in the dirt immediately. On a cool day, rub your pet with towels and then walk him. If he is still damp, put the blanket on him and push handsful of straw up under the blanket to keep it away from his back so the air can circulate.

BATHING

You will probably want to bathe your horse sometime—either before a show, after a hard ride on a hot day, or just on some warm afternoon when you feel like giving your pet the works.

It is not necessary to bathe your horse often, because daily grooming will keep his coat quite healthy. Instead of frequent allover baths, spot-wash any white areas that get stained. Bathing a horse removes dandruff, dirt, and manure stains, but it also removes the natural oil from the coat so it will not be as glossy for a day or two.

Do not wash your horse in cold weather, and try to do it at least two days before a show. If you do bathe your horse the day before a show, use a coat conditioner afterward to bring out the sheen again.

1. If there is a hose available, attach to it a rubber or plastic currycomb made for this purpose and rub in a circular motion, with the water running, to draw out the dirt next to your horse's skin.

2. Mix up a pail of warm water and antibacterial soap and, with your third or body sponge, wash around the horse's face and ears. Wring out the sponge so the soapy water doesn't drip into his eyes or ears. Rinse.

3. Start at the top of the horse's neck again and scrub with the sponge to remove any stains. Wash a section (neck and chest) at a time, working the soap up into a good lather. Rinse as you go, so the soap isn't left on too long to dry out the horse's skin.

4. Wash the mane, brushing it over to the right or off side with the stiff dandy brush if you ride your horse English style. Then do the tail, dipping the whole thing into the bucket so you can really dig down to the bone to

Instead of frequent allover baths, spot-wash any white areas that get stained

clean it. Rinse it well and use the dandy brush and then comb to untangle it. A plastic comb won't break the hair as a metal one does.

5. Last, wash the horse's lower legs and then the hoofs. Rinse your horse off well, either with a hose or several pails of water. Use the sweat scraper to scrape off any excess water on his body, not on the face or legs. Dry the face with a clean towel and walk the horse until he dries completely.

Hoof dressing may be applied to the hoofs once or twice a week to keep them pliable and to improve their appearance before a show. Do not put it on more often, because too much will have the opposite effect and seal moisture out.

A mane on an English horse that won't stay down on the right side should be brushed over to the correct side every time you groom him. One that refuses to stay in place can be weighted down with Dippity-do or sponged, braided, and left pulled over for a day or two. Watch your horse to see that it doesn't irritate. If it does, the animal will rub his neck to get the braids out and rub off chunks of the mane, too.

Never cut your horse's mane with a scissors except over the poll where the bridle goes. To shorten a mane, it has to be "pulled" by backcombing a small section and then pulling out the 3 to 6 longest hairs remaining in your fingers. It doesn't hurt if you don't pull too many at one time.

Some Western horses have their manes roached except for the forelock and a handhold at the withers. This must be done with clippers, up one side of the neck, up the other, and then up the middle.

Before using electric clippers on your horse, turn them on and hold them next to the animal for a few minutes every day to get your pet used to their sound and looks. Make sure they are sharp and clean so they don't catch and pull the hair.

Trimming is a job for an expert, and clipping out the ears, around the fetlocks, and under the jaw is not a simple job. Have someone show you how before you take a chunk out of your horse's ear and make the animal clipper-shy forever.

A horse that is kept blanketed during the winter will not have so heavy a coat. Even so, by spring a one- or two-handled shedding blade will come in handy to scrape off the mass of loose hair. Use it lightly on the flanks and stomach and not at all on the face or lower legs.

Keep your grooming equipment all together in a bucket, old trunk, or box, on a shelf, or in the compartments of an old shoebag. Don't drop tools underfoot while you groom, because you or your horse may step on them. Put them away after you use them and they will never be "missing."

HOOFS

A horse's feet and their care are a very important part of horse hygiene. Feet should be kept clean and not allowed to dry out. They should be trimmed and shod when shoes are necessary for riding on hard surfaces.

Hoofs should be trimmed every four to six weeks by a competent blacksmith

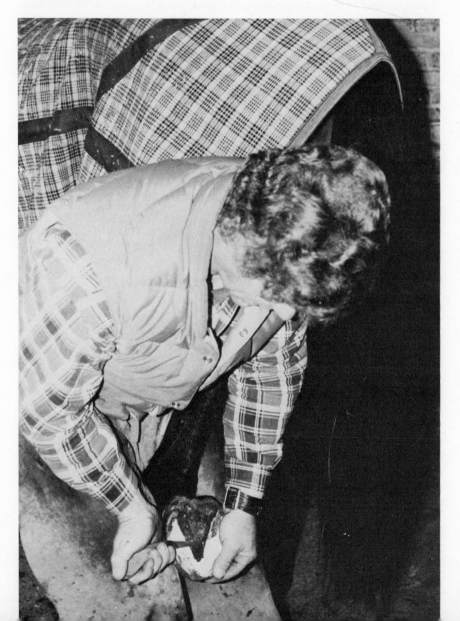

A horse who cannot put any weight on an injured or sore foot will not be able to walk, because a horse cannot limp as a dog or cat can.

Clean a stabled or worked horse's feet daily, checking for loose shoes or thrush. Thrush is a disease of the foot caused by a damp, dirty stall or paddock. It is noticeable by the foul odor coming from the infected foot or feet. Thrush will make your horse lame and can be very serious if not treated.

Hoofs should be trimmed every four to six weeks, whether your horse is shod or not. They grow just as your fingernails do, and if not trimmed, will cause such problems as toeing in or out, and even altering the way your horse moves, putting unnatural stress on his legs.

Shoes should be reset every four to six weeks by a competent black-smith. They should be made to fit the foot and not the reverse—the foot to fit the shoe.

Shoes are used to change gaits, correct faulty hoof structure or growth, and aid a hoof that has corns, contracted heels, or cracks. Leather pads and shoes with borium give horses better traction on roads and in ice and snow.

Many horsemen believe that a horse's feet should be given a rest and allowed to go unshod for a couple of months. Depending on your climate, a good time for this might be in the winter, when cold weather keeps you indoors. It won't hurt to ride your horse occasionally if the ground is soft or covered with snow. However, regular trimming is still necessary during this time.

In 1976 trimming cost $5 to $8, resetting old shoes $15 to $18, and shoeing with new shoes $20 to $25, depending on the area you live in and how far the blacksmith has to travel.

CLEANING STALLS

Cleaning stalls strengthens your muscles, builds character, and clears out your sinuses, according to one longtime horse owner. If you cheat on stall-cleaning, it will eventually catch up with you and then you'll really have a big job to do.

Stalls that are cleaned daily are more healthful for your horse and easier and more economical for you to maintain. The easiest way to clean your horse's stall is to do it when he is outside.

1. Pick up all the wet bedding and droppings with the manure fork and shovel, and put it in the wheelbarrow or manure basket. Save as much dry bedding as you can.

2. Pitch the rest of the bedding out to the sides of the stall, where it can dry. Leave the floor uncovered during the day, so it will dry out, too.

3. Sprinkle lime on a clay, wood, or dirt floor and wash an asphalt or cement one with disinfectant once a week. Don't let your horse get to it. A good layer of bedding over the lime and a thorough rinsing of the disinfectant before the horse is put in his stall will prevent this.

4. Sweep the aisles, tack room, and other areas in your barn for a neater appearance and to keep loose hay and straw from spreading or starting a fire.

5. If your horse is to be inside, you should pick up his droppings at least three times during the day.

6. In the evening, push the old bedding back into the center and add fresh to it. Separate and toss the fresh bedding around with your hands or a pitchfork.

Bedding should be deep enough—8 to 12 inches, if straw—for a horse to lie in comfortably. You should use more in winter for warmth.

Turn your horse out as much as possible and you won't have to use as much bedding and will have less cleaning to do. Your horse need only come into the barn on cold winter nights or hot summer days.

LONGEING

Longeing is an excellent way to give your horse his daily exercise if you are short of time and unable to ride. It's also a great warm-up before riding to get the kinks and bucks out of your mount. Twenty minutes is long enough for a warm-up, and thirty minutes is sufficient if you won't be riding.

Attach a long line to the halter's ring under the chin. Walk your horse in a small circle, gradually giving him more line, so that you are making an even smaller circle as he walks around you on the outside.

Keep moving backward to the center, giving him more line until you are turning in place. A long whip, usually just shown to him or waved at him, not for hitting, will keep him out. As he gets the idea, you can let out more line until the circle is larger.

If he starts to come in to you, wave the whip in his face. You may have to start over a few times before he gets the idea.

Never allow him to walk into the center when you wish to stop or change directions. Instead, you go out to him. If, after several attempts, he still doesn't understand what you want him to do, have a friend lead him around you in a circle until he does. If this fails, and he still will not do what you want, stop and try again the next day.

After he has been walking around you in a circle on his own for a while, you may start him trotting. Crack or wave the whip and tell him, "Trot." Say the commands, "Trot," "Walk," or "Whoa" very clearly and with authority. With practice he will change gaits on voice commands alone.

When he has learned to walk, trot, and halt in both directions, you may start him cantering. This is a little more difficult, because you will also have to get him on the correct lead.

Do not make your horse go around and around in the same direction, or he will become bored and you dizzy. Keep the circles a good size and change directions frequently, so the pressure isn't on the muscles of his inside leg only.

Don't wrap the line around your hand or waist to take up the slack. If something should startle him, he could turn and run, dragging you if you can't get loose. Wear gloves to prevent blisters if your horse pulls or jerks on the line.

7
HORSE ETIQUETTE

A well-mannered horse is a pleasure to own. A spoiled, nasty animal is untrustworthy, no fun, and potentially dangerous.

Choose a friendly, gentle horse to live in your backyard, or one with only minor vices that patience and understanding can correct. Most bad habits are the result of poor training or bad handling by a previous owner.

Treat your horse with consideration and kindness. If you shove a winter-cold bit into your horse's mouth or burn his tongue on a bit left out in the hot sun, your pet will begin to fight you every time you try to put on the bridle. If you jerk the girth tight when saddling the horse, the animal will learn to relieve the pinching "punch" by blowing up or expanding his barrel, an annoying habit, impossible to break once learned.

When you correct your horse, discipline firmly, but not cruelly, with a stern "No," a sharp whack, or both. Prolonged beating or whipping will only frighten him and may even ingrain the action into a repertoire of tricks.

Correct your horse immediately after he disobeys you or tries some shenanigan. Even a moment later will be too late. Your horse will connect punishment with behavior immediately preceding it.

Never pit your muscles against those of your horse. Superior strength will win the tug-of-war every time. Instead, use your head to make your horse do what you want—brains over brawn.

A HORSE'S MAKEUP

The horse has been a faithful companion to man for centuries. The animal's strength, speed, and stamina have been valuable and useful ever since he became domesticated. The horse has taken a place alongside man throughout history—helping to fight, trying to win sports, working to tame

Do not jerk the girth tight when saddling your horse

frontiers, pulling the plow to till land, and carrying his master, often for only an hour or two, away from civilization's tensions and headaches into nature's peace and beauty.

A horse is naturally skittish and timid. Flight, rather than fight, was the horse's defense against its predators during the years of evolution, and this is still a very strong instinct. Every impulse tells a horse to turn and run at the slightest danger—or what may seem dangerous. Sometimes this is a rock, a puddle's reflection, a rabbit hopping across the path, or a sheet flapping on a clothesline.

A horse that shies should be reassured, not punished. Angry words and blows will only frighten the animal more.

Another tendency, dating back into the horse's past, is the desire to remain with the herd. A horse dislikes being alone, and if there are no other horses around, he will be happier with a stablemate, such as a cat, rabbit, donkey, goat, or even a chicken.

Some horses are so herd-bound that it is almost impossible to ride them away from the barn or out on a trail without the company of other horses. They know that there is safety in numbers and will refuse to leave their fellow equines. You must build up their confidence and work on going out alone to encourage their boldness.

Horses are not big dogs, with the intellect and devotion of a canine. They are horses, in spite of what some people will try to tell you. However, they are far smarter than most animals and with repetition and competent training can be taught to do many things: cutting a steer out of the rest of the herd, unnatural gaits like the rack, dressage movements, holding the rope taut after a calf has been roped, circus tricks, or just carrying a rider.

Horses are rarely devoted to people. Some whinny when their owners approach, nuzzle them with obvious affection, or come when they are called, but most transfer such actions to whoever next feeds and cares for them. A few really do seem to care for their owner, but the horse's familiarity with and confidence in that person are a probable explanation.

As with most species, horses have individual personalities. Some are definitely "people horses" and are more responsive to people. Others exhibit a strong desire to lead, whether they are in a horse race or on a trail ride. Still others—and not necessarily the biggest and strongest—dominate their companions when turned out in a field.

Some horses love to jump. Some enjoy strutting in front of a horse show audience, and others are content to plod happily along behind their comrades. A horse's makeup usually depends on age, sex, breeding, and temperament.

CONTRIBUTING TO VICES

As mentioned before, most vices that horses have are caused by their owners.

A horse that nips may have been fed by hand—carrots, apples, sugar

—whenever his owner approached him. A tidbit as a reward is acceptable, but try to give it to your horse in the feed bin. A horse that expects constant handouts will become annoyed when they're not given and nip to remind you.

Never teach your horse to find the "goody" in your pocket or to accept it from between your teeth. A nip on the hip by a frustrated horse who is attempting to retrieve a carrot from your pocket is painful, but hardly as disfiguring as the loss of the tip of your nose. This tragedy actually happened at a local stable to one young lady who was old enough to know better.

Be especially careful what tricks you intentionally teach your horse. Teaching him to stand quietly when being tacked up or mounted, to lift his feet one at a time to be cleaned, or to come when he is called, are practical and helpful, but some circus-type antics may cause unnecessary accidents.

Do not teach your horse to rear on a given signal. You may think you look like the Lone Ranger on Silver, but if your pet ever rears suddenly or loses his balance and goes over backward, you may turn up looking like Frankenstein's mummy encased in a wad of bandages.

Pawing the ground to tell his age may start your horse pawing in his stall or pawing anywhere he is standing.

Let the instructors at the Spanish Riding School in Vienna teach caprioles, levades, and courbettes to their beautiful white Lipizzans. You stick to everyday stable etiquette.

VICES AND HOW TO COPE WITH THEM

Often a horse disobeys because of not knowing what is expected. Even a well-trained horse can be confused if the correct signal is not given.

If you discover why a horse has a particular habit or performs a certain action, you are halfway to the solution. Many horses pick up vices, such as *cribbing* (wood-chewing), *weaving, wind sucking,* or *kicking the walls,* because they are bored from standing all day in their stalls. The simplest solutions include turning them out more often, giving them additional exercise, hanging a ball or plastic milk jug in their stall for them to bat around,

A horse is happier with a stable companion

or doling out their daily hay in several small portions to keep them occupied longer rather than in one or two big feedings. A collar may have to be used on a confirmed windsucker, and metal pieces or nasty-tasting paints put on all exposed wood to discourage a wood chewer.

If your horse *blows up* when his girth is tightened, take the girth up by degrees, a notch or two. Then walk him outside, where he will let the air go, and tighten it again.

If your horse *refuses to stand* while you are mounting, have someone hold the bridle at first. Work up to mounting by yourself with the horse headed into the corner of a wall or fence and then finally anywhere. Practice getting on and off, always praising when the horse stands. Make sure, when you mount, that you are not poking your horse in the belly with your toe. This will certainly cause fidgeting.

After mounting, adjust your stirrups, reins, and girth while making your horse stand still so your pet learns not to move off as soon as you have swung your leg over his back. Other riders in your group should wait until you have mounted before starting. No horse will stand still if the others are leaving him.

If your horse *bites,* punish him immediately on the nose or neck with a slap that is hard enough to hurt. Loudly scold him at the same time. If you don't let him know that you dislike such actions, the animal may really hurt you someday. However, never hit your pet on the head, as this will cause head shying.

As previously mentioned, a horse that *rears* should be quickly discouraged from doing so. Some trainers say to spin the horse in a circle when you feel him start to rear. Hitting on the head, once thought to cure this bad habit, usually only makes the horse wilder and more uncontrollable. Calming and talking now prove to have better results.

If your horse does rear, lean as far forward as you can and let the reins go slack, so you don't pull him over backward. Check for a too-small bit or bridle, or teeth that should be filed, before you condemn your horse altogether.

Your horse should stand quietly with his head down when being bridled

A horse that *refuses to be led* is rare, but there are some that walk into you, pull back on the lead, or toss their heads, yanking the rope out of your hands. Always lead from the left or near side with your right hand on the lead rope about 8 to 10 inches from the halter and your left hand holding the slack. Turn your horse by pushing the animal around away from you. Never pull the horse toward you unless you want to risk having your toes stepped on.

Walk briskly beside your horse. Never walk backward in front of the animal. Many horses will stop and refuse to move if you are facing them. Do not wrap the lead rope around your wrist or hand.

A horse that *eats bedding,* the walls of the stall, or even his own manure may have a mineral deficiency, worms, or not enough bulk food (hay). These habits may also be caused by boredom or just plain hunger pangs if the horse is not fed enough.

If your horse *kicks,* tie the animal in crossties when you are grooming him, and do not walk too closely behind. A horse that does kick out should be smacked sharply on the hindquarters. Swishing the tail and laying the ears back are signals that another kick may be coming.

If you have a horse that *puts his head down* to graze every chance he gets, or snatches leaves from trees along the trail, you should be ready to correct him every time. Keep a firm grip on the reins, but not too heavy a pressure on his mouth. If the horse does succeed in snatching a mouthful, say "No" immediately and smack his rump. Expect a startled jump.

Don't allow your horse to *use you as a scratching post* for a hot itchy head after riding. "No" and a slap on the neck can save you quite a cleaning bill and possibly even a hard knock on the head. After you have untacked your horse, be sure to rub around the ears and mouth with a towel to relieve discomfort.

Hard to catch in the field? Set up your routine so you will be bringing in your horse at feeding time. Have feed waiting in the stall. Once the animal realizes that the sooner come, the sooner fed, you will have a horse trotting in at your first whistle.

If your horse attempts to bully you by *turning his rump toward whoever enters the stall,* or trying to *crowd* you into the wall, you should encourage the animal to face you by offering a handful of oats or other tidbit. If this doesn't work, give a whack with the lead rope or a crop, but be prepared for a kick in return. Then repeat the procedure until the horse finally faces you. Reward success with praise and feed.

In the horse world there is rarely only one way to do something. What works with one horse may not work with another. If your horse's manners have not improved after a reasonable length of time, try a different method of correction. Patience, stick-to-itiveness, and time are the healing agents.

Your horse will be easier to catch if you bring him in at feeding time

TRAILERING

Someday you may have to van your horse to another destination, whether it is to a horse show, another riding area, a friend's barn, or a new home. If you have a horse that loads easily and rides contentedly and calmly, you won't have any problem.

However, if your horse is afraid of or unaccustomed to a van, start making it familiar to him slowly, well in advance of "moving day." If you have your own trailer, park it with its door open in the horse's field so the animal can inspect it at leisure. Place his hay on the ramp, and each day move the hay a little farther up into the van so the horse has to step onto the ramp to reach it.

The van should be a sturdy, safe one—no open truck or homemade trailer with too steep a ramp. Matting or bedding should be put on a smooth trailer floor for better footing. The van should be checked regularly by an experienced mechanic, meet all state regulations, and display more than adequate brake and taillights. Before driving, all connections (lights, brakes, hitch, and safety chains) should be checked, and all doors closed. Check them again at every stop.

When loading, talk to your horse and lead him in slowly up the middle of the tail gate, so feet cannot slip off. The ground around the van should have good footing. Make sure there is plenty of headroom, and don't try to squeeze a large horse into a too-small van. Have a hay net or manger full and waiting. Put the sun at your horse's back, shining into the van, so the animal isn't walking into a dark, cavelike structure that may be scary.

If you are vanning only one horse, put the animal on the driver's side of the van or the inside of the road or crown to lessen the chance of tipping. If you have two horses, put the biggest or heaviest on the inside.

Loading a trailer should be done by two persons, unless your horse is trained to walk into the trailer alone so you only have to hook the chain behind. Rather than getting in front of the horse and leading the animal in, you should stand on one side of the center divider in a two-horse trailer and lead your horse into the other.

Avoid rushing or pulling—the horse is much stronger than you, and one unhappy incident will make the animal wary of any trailer forever. For a hesitant horse, have two assistants hold a rope across the rump, even with the base of the tailbone, and gently push the horse forward. You offer encouragement with some oats. As soon as the animal is in place, immedi-

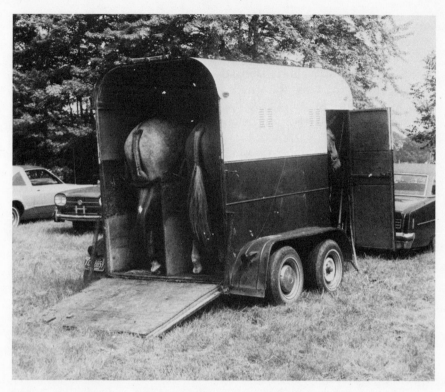

You may want to van your horse someday, so acquaint him with the trailer beforehand

ately snap the chain behind him and close the door or tail gate, so the horse can't fly out backward, breaking the chain or going under it.

Then tie and reward the horse with a handful of grain or a carrot. Always stand to one side of a horse, never directly behind or in front when loading or unloading.

A horse that is more stubborn than afraid can be whacked with the bristle end of a broom as persuasion to step lively.

If you are trailering two horses, load the experienced, calmer one first to reassure the other horse. Horses should always be tied by their halters with a quick release knot inside the van.

Make your horse's first ride a short, slow one with a competent driver and with as little fuss and as few other people involved as possible. Try to arrange the feeding schedule so the horse is not full of feed and water and thus more apt to suffer from motion sickness. It is against the law for anyone to ride in the van with a horse, and a driver should never travel over 50 mph, keeping double or triple the length of the van between his and the next vehicle. Sudden stops and starts, and sharp turns may cause a horse to lose footing. This can be avoided by defensive driving, looking far ahead to avoid emergencies.

A horse that has trouble keeping his feet while riding alone in a trailer can be helped if you remove the center partition so feet can spread for better balance.

If a horse is nervous and kicks the sides of the van, wrap the legs to protect them. Use plenty of padding under the bandage and cover the legs from the knee down to well over the top of the hoof. This is a good idea even with horses that ride well. To save time, you can use zip-on bandages.

Tail wraps are for those horses that sit on the tail gate. Check to see if the tail is inside the van. Some horses particularly dislike their tails blowing in the wind.

To unload, untie your horse through the front or escape door first, toss the lead rope over his neck, open the back door and unhook the tail chain. Have someone guide the animal down the ramp and grab the lead rope after you have started him out by putting your hand on his chest with the command, "Back." It is safer to have no other tack than the halter on.

To accustom a green horse to vanning—loading and unloading—try it even when you are not going anywhere. Feed hay inside so the horse gets used to the surroundings. Practice makes perfect.

8
HORSE SENSE ON THE TRAILS

Trail riding for most of today's backyard horse owners frequently becomes a jog along public roads, around farmers' fields, and past neighbors' lawns. But whether your ride is through the heavily developed areas of suburbia or through the woods and meadows of a more rural countryside, common sense and common courtesy are necessary for your own and your horse's safety and for continued permission to ride on private property.

PLAN AHEAD

Before participating in a trail ride—whether an all-day outing or an hour's trot around the block—take into consideration your ability to ride and the condition of both yourself and your horse. To prepare for longer, more strenuous trips, work yourself and your horse into shape with shorter jaunts at first. Although the actual ride may not be tiring, especially if your horse is walking most of the time, for the next couple of days afterward you'll feel muscles you never knew you had.

For trail riding choose a steady, reliable mount, not one that is highstrung and easily excited. The snorting steed with the flashing eyes and prancing walk may capture your admiration, but be worthless and actually dangerous on a narrow mountain trail when a rabbit darts from the bushes under his nose.

Know your horse and his habits or peculiarities. If your mount tends to shy at rotting stumps and protruding boulders, or at just the hollow sound of his own hoofbeats on a wooden bridge, be prepared as you pass by or over one of these "scary monsters." A sudden side jump or reverse may cause you to lose your balance. Your horse's mood on the day of your ride will also signal to you how brave or flighty he will be when encountering nature's wonders and man's inventions.

Your tack and your horse should be inspected before you start out on any ride. A broken saddle girth or a thrown shoe can mean a long walk home.

Wipe your horse down with fly repellent before taking a summer ride through the woods. It will discourage the mosquitoes and deerflies that buzz about your horse's ears and settle on the back of your neck.

Tie long or light-colored tails into a mud knot by braiding the strands, twisting them into a knot, and fastening them with yarn or cord to make the cleaning of your mount much easier after a ride on muddy trails. This will also eliminate much of the staining that yellow or red clay and just plain dirt can do to a white, cream, or gray tail. Unlike the precise tail-braiding on a jumper or hunter before a show or fox hunt, the mud knot is not meant to be a thing of beauty, but a creation of convenience. Any intertwining that will stay in place the length of your ride will do.

Clean your horse thoroughly before saddling and bridling him. Even a few grains of caked mud under the saddle can cause a painful sore. Make sure the saddle pad is smooth, because wrinkles in it can also rub your horse's back raw. Tighten the girth by degrees rather than with a sudden jerk, checking to see that it is sufficiently secured before you mount. Nothing is more embarrassing than trying to mount and landing on your backside with the saddle slipped halfway around the horse's belly.

Mounting should not be done in the barn or near a fence. A cracked head or slashed leg may be the result of poor distance judging. To spare the horse's back try to mount easily and lightly, not like a sack of potatoes.

OUT ON THE TRAILS

Most riding is done in a single file because trails are usually not wide enough for more than one horse. The lead horse should be trailwise and aggressive. A fearful animal will be a problem if he must be the first to walk through streams and past unfamiliar objects. A horse will generally do whatever the other horses in the group do. A horse that jumps or bolts at every movement in the underbrush will be an unsuitable leader, because the horses behind will imitate every move, jumping or bolting almost simultaneously.

Horses that tend to kick should be last in line. Many owners tie a red ribbon to a kicker's tail to warn other riders to keep their distance. Old-timers often say, "Walk your horse the first half mile out and the last mile

Tighten the girth by degrees rather than with a sudden jerk

in.'' This is good advice: your horse may be tight after standing for hours in a stall, and the slower pace will give the animal a chance to limber up. The end of that first half mile is also a good time to stop and check your girth.

Whether you are walking along a heavily traveled highway, cantering down a path through an overgrown field, or maneuvering a steep, rocky trail through dense woods, the most important rule is to have your mount under control at all times. In some circumstances, an experienced horse knows how to handle obstacles better than an inexperienced rider, and at such moments, give your mount his head, but never the upper hand. A pheasant may suddenly fly up in his face, and steady reins will be needed to calm him.

GROUND SURFACES—WHEN TO WALK, TROT, OR CANTER

Various ground surfaces can cause problems for trail riders. Mudholes and boggy areas should be avoided whenever possible. If you must travel through them, walk your horse. Mud is very slippery and the suction from it can even pull a shoe off. Boggy areas in which you think your horse might sink should be tested first. Dismount and step onto the surface yourself to determine how deep your horse may go down. If, as you progress through the bog, he starts to panic or scramble wildly, try to keep him calm or he may pull a muscle.

If freezing is predicted later in the day or evening, the ruts made by your horse's hoofs will harden into uneven footing—rough going for horses on succeeding days, and another reason to avoid muddy areas on trails.

Snow, too, deserves respect when riding through it. Hard balls of ice can build up in your horse's feet and actually seem to put the animal on ice skates. Walking on ice-caked hoofs through snow and over ice gives a horse very little traction.

Horses without shoes should be kept off hard surfaces, or their feet will soon become tender and sore. Roadways of gravel and small stones may also be hazardous, because pebbles can get stuck in a horse's foot and cause painful bruises.

Even if your horse is shod, travel at a walk or slow trot on paved roads. The hard surface can inflict many kinds of leg and foot ailments. Unless a horse has borium on his shoes (similar to studs on a car's tires), paved roads can be almost as slippery as ice because of the oil deposited by passing cars. If you think there is a chance that your horse might fall, remove your feet from the stirrups so that you can jump free.

Riding on heavily traveled roads should be avoided, but, if it is neces-sary, ride in a single file on the right-hand side of the road as far from the traffic as possible. Some riders prefer the left-hand side, as pedestrians do, so that their horses can see the oncoming traffic. However, a large truck roaring toward your horse may cause him to shy suddenly, possibly tossing you into the truck's path.

In many areas horses still have the right of way, but since there are more cars than horses, challenging vehicles in the middle of a busy intersec-tion is not advisable. Always look before crossing a road—be it country lane or interstate highway.

Be twice as cautious if you are riding along a road at night. Wear light-colored clothes and put reflecting tape on your horse. If your mount will tolerate it, cut a piece of white sheeting to drape over the hindquarters. Stick reflecting tape on it and attach it to the cantle of your saddle for added protection.

If your horse is apprehensive about an approaching vehicle, turn to face it as it passes. Do this in a driveway or wider area along the road, so you both are out of the path of oncoming traffic. A horse facing the frightening object will be less likely to bolt.

Wave down speeding motorists so that they slow up when passing, and always thank considerate drivers.

Cantering or galloping across a strange field is foolhardy if you don't keep a sharp lookout. An unexpected hole, dug by a groundhog, mole, or other small animal, may cause serious injuries to both you and your horse if your mount steps into it. Watch for mounds of soft dirt, for they will often signal the existence of such holes.

Be wary when crossing or going through a fence that is down. Barbed wire and postholes are often hidden by heavy brush.

Before taking an unfamiliar jump, check the footing and clearance on the other side. Don't jump while trail riding alone if you and your horse lack experience and training. A phone and help may be too far away if you fall and injure yourself.

Watch for bottles, cans, and broken glass discarded by our "throwa-way society," because they can give your mount a nasty cut. Warn the riders behind you to prevent their horses from stepping on them, too.

Streams and puddles mean different things to different horses. To some they look inviting and to others they are terrifying. Either way, make your horse walk through them. Don't allow him to jump, or he may end up on the rump of the horse in front or sink up to the knees in mud on the opposite bank.

If your horse stops in midstream and begins to paw, kick him on. This is often a signal that he is planning to roll.

If the horse is frightened, keep him moving, but do so gently and reassure him repeatedly. Don't tense up or try to force him into the water, as this will only cause more fright. A more courageous horse in front can help to lead others across, and a sniff and a few sips may also convince them that this liquid is just like the water in the pail back home.

While you are crossing, watch out for branches floating downstream that may strike against and twist between your horse's legs. Feeling much like snakes, the branches may prompt a leap forward and perhaps a slip on moss-covered rocks, giving you a bad spill.

When meeting steep banks, your horse will be able to jump up or down those that rise less than three feet or half his height. A gradual slope may be climbed or slid down. On a decline, always walk your horse to avoid slipping down against the horse in front. Your mount's body should be straight, hindquarters in line with forehead. Push your feet just far enough in front of you so that the stirrup leathers remain vertical to the ground, and keep the reins loose, allowing the horse freedom of head and neck. Do not try to hold him up.

Going uphill, lean forward, standing up out of the saddle so that your weight is over the horse's shoulders. Grab the mane to pull yourself up and help to maintain your balance.

Trotting downhill, don't attempt to post, but stand slightly in your stirrups. It's easier on you and the horse. For long canters or gallops, again stand slightly in your stirrups, leaning forward. The hand gallop position is not so tiring and will conserve your energy.

If you must ride through a heavily developed area, be ready for anything. A door opening suddenly, a barking dog, or a flapping sheet on a clothesline can unnerve even the sturdiest, quietest horse.

POLITENESS COUNTS

Trail-riding manners should always be practiced for your own and your fellow riders' safety. Through hand or voice signals warn those behind you of any change in gait. Never ride too close to the horse in front of you, or the latter may become irritated and kick you or your mount, possibly unseating his own rider at the same time.

Don't try to hold branches out of the way of the rider behind you. Your arms just aren't long enough to hold them until the next rider can reach them. Just push around them and try not to let them snap back into another rider or his horse's face.

If you plan on riding through private property, permission should be obtained first. Consideration should be shown toward the owners of the land over which you are riding. Always close any gates that you have to open to pass through. No rancher will appreciate having to round up loose cattle. Think of the farmers, too, by not scaring their livestock or riding

Always walk your horse through a stream

through their cultivated fields. A horse's hoofs can chop down young plants, ruining a large portion of the crops.

Keep to the trails, so that you don't trample wild flowers, delicate ground cover, lawns, or gardens. Remember that you and your horse are guests on someone else's property. Careless destruction will cause generous owners to close their land to horses and riders.

A PAUSE BY THE WAYSIDE

Stopping for lunch or a break may be necessary and welcome to all those taking part in a long trail ride. Upon dismounting, loosen the girth and run your stirrups up. Tether your horse by a halter or a neck rope—never by the bridle, for one good jerk can easily break it, resulting in costly repairs.

Tie your horse by a halter or a neck rope—never by the bridle

Be sure your mount is cooled down. Never let a hot horse stand or drink water.

Tie your horse to a branch no lower than his shoulder height so that he can't get his head down and the rope around his legs. Use a knot that can be untied quickly in an emergency, and separate the horses so that they cannot kick or bite each other. If you leave the bridle on, loop the reins behind the raised stirrups so that they're out of the horse's way. Tie the horses where you can see them, so that any problems can be noticed immediately.

Before leaving the picnic area, clean up your rubbish and dispose of it in receptacles or, if none are available, take it home with you. Extinguish fires completely with water, dirt, or sand.

See that girths are tightened and bridles on correctly before you continue your ride.

HOME AGAIN

As you near the barn, keep your horses at a walk, even though they may want to pick up their pace. Galloping home is an easy way to lose control of your mount and to receive a good crack on the head as the horse charges into a low-beamed barn. Walking the last mile home is also an excellent way of cooling your horse off without a lot of walking around on foot later.

Common sense and courtesy combined with a little "horse sense" should guarantee you many pleasant days of trail riding. One last bit of advice: Stay alert and always expect the unexpected.

9
IS THERE A HORSE DOCTOR IN THE HOUSE?

Even the healthiest horses get sick, but to lessen the chances of its happening to your horse, practice preventive measures—regular inoculations and worming as well as daily grooming, feeding, and barn-cleaning.

Conscientious care is a lot easier and less expensive than having to nurse a horse back to good health. Just not being able to ride because the horse is getting over an injury or illness is a nuisance.

As soon as you buy a horse, a preventive medical program should be set up with your veterinarian and should include vaccinations for influenza and encephalomyelitis (sleeping sickness), a permanent tetanus immunization with annual boosters, a Coggins test for equine infectious anemia, and semi-annual wormings. There is the real possibility that neglect in planning such a program could cause the animal's death.

Although a veterinarian should be called promptly at the first sign of difficulty—listlessness, coughing, unusual lumps or swellings, runny nose and eyes, heat in the legs or feet, or lack of interest in food—there are treatments for minor ills and injuries that every horse-owning family should know. To be able to perform this type of first aid you must have in your horse's medicine cabinet:

a blunt-ended veterinary
   rectal thermometer

boric acid powder
   for washing eyes

sterile cotton and gauze bandages

petroleum jelly

antiseptic dusting powder

iodine (tincture of)

epsom salts

methylene blue

bluestone (copper sulphate)

blunt-ended scissors

Regular inoculations help to keep horses healthy

worm medicine (as prescribed)	topical ointment
liniment	rubbing alcohol
colic remedy (as prescribed)	a dose syringe for liquid medicine

Many of these can be acquired as you need them. In time, your cabinet will be overflowing with lotions, powders, and ointments. Be sure to use only those your veterinarian recommends for a particular illness or injury. The wrong medicine may lead to serious complications.

Bring all medicines into your house during the winter so that they do not freeze.

FIRST AID

Every horse is an individual, just as each person is. What one mare does may be perfectly normal for her, but for another the same behavior may be the first stage of some illness. Know your horse so you can determine whether that afternoon nap, half-eaten feed, or loose bowel movement is typical or means trouble.

The average number of bowel movements of an average healthy horse is eight each day, but, like all estimates, this will depend on the individual horse.

The normal temperature for a horse is from 100.2° to 100.5° Fahrenheit (37.8 to 38.1 C.), 103° F. (39.4 C.), indicates a moderately high fever, and anything over 106° F. (41.1 C.) is dangerous.

If you think your horse has a temperature, check with the veterinarian promptly.

Puncture wounds, such as those caused by a nail, should be washed clean with warm water and soap, opened so they will drain, and cleaned with disinfectant. Then dust the wound with antiseptic powder and leave it uncovered. If your horse has not already received the annual tetanus shot, call your vet immediately.

Abrasions, such as those caused by rubbing a tail during shipping, should be smeared with petroleum jelly. Saddle and girth sores require being painted with methylene blue several times daily. No riding should be allowed until these are completely healed.

Cuts from barbed wire or glass should be kept clean, and tincture of iodine or a topical ointment should be put on them. If there is severe bleeding, your vet must be called to see whether stitching is necessary.

Rope burns usually respond to methylene blue. You should try to get them to heal without a scab if they are located below the fetlock, because the scabs will crack open whenever the horse moves.

If a leg artery is slashed, the blood will spurt and you must put on a tourniquet, making sure to release it every fifteen minutes to avoid gangrene. If the slashed artery is on the body, apply pressure between the wound and the heart, feeling around until you find the place that reduces the flow best. If a vein is cut, the blood will flow and you must apply pressure on the side of the wound away from the heart. Do not use a tourniquet.

Cold compresses will slow down the blood flow of minor wounds, but do not cover a bleeding wound immediately, because the flow will wash away any germs. Infection sets in easily, so watch the wound and surrounding area for danger signs: swelling, soreness, excessive heat, and, a few days later, a pus discharge.

COMMON AILMENTS

The most common horse ailments are colic, the common cold, flu, respiratory diseases, and lameness. You should be able to recognize their symptoms, know when to call your veterinarian, and be able to help your horse until the vet arrives.

Colic refers to the abdominal pain produced by various abnormal conditions in the bowels, such as gas or a ball of undigested food blocking the intestines. The horse's one-way digestive system makes it impossible to vomit as a cat or dog does, and anything harmful to him must be rejected through elimination. Because of this system, a horse is particularly susceptible to forage poisoning or botulism, brought about most often by consuming spoiled grain. It can also occur if your horse eats poisonous weeds sometimes found in hay or even lurking in your pasture.

Colic contributes to more deaths in horses than any other single illness.

Cause: Poor feeding procedures, such as overfeeding, feeding when the horse is hot or excited, or feeding spoiled or moldy food.

Symptoms: A horse with colic will break out in a sweat, bite or kick at his side, paw the ground, and try to lie down and roll.

Treatment: Call your vet immediately and follow instructions until the vet arrives. Usually you will be told to give a dose of colic medicine, get your horse on his feet and walk him. He can twist his intestines if allowed to lie down and roll.

Coughs and colds, to which young horses are particularly susceptible, are similar to those in people.

Symptoms: Nasal discharge, nagging cough, high temperature, lack of appetite, and spiritlessness.

Treatment: Keep your horse warm and well blanketed. Feed a hot bran mash (see Chapter 5) once a day, allow plenty of rest, and give whatever medication your vet prescribes. Colds are contagious, so isolate your horse from others for the ten to fourteen days of the illness.

Prevention: Do not put your horse away hot. Cool him out thoroughly after riding. Do not leave him standing in drafts, or allow him to get overtired or chilled.

Equine influenza, or the flu, is contacted usually by young animals, but is rarely fatal.

Symptoms: A high temperature (as much as 106° F., 41.1 C., for two to ten days), loss of appetite, weakness, rapid breathing, a dry cough, and a watery discharge from eyes and nostrils.

Treatment: Isolation and rest are recommended until the temperature and cough diminish.

Prevention: Your horse should be vaccinated about a month before he comes into contact with other horses, such as at a horse show. Usually two injections are given two to four weeks apart, and then an annual booster.

Shipping fever, also known as distemper, is a highly contagious upper respiratory disease.

Symptoms: A high temperature and loss of appetite, followed by a nasal discharge and a swelling and probable abscessing of the lymph nodes under the jaw. The infection runs its course in two to four weeks.

Treatment: Your veterinarian will treat the bacteria, usually with antibiotics, and will tell you how to deal with any abscesses. Your horse should be isolated, if possible, given complete rest, fresh drinking water, and light feeds like bran mashes. He should be kept out of drafts.

Lameness may be caused by thrush or founder (laminitis), among numerous other possibilities. Thrush causes the frog of the hoof to become rotten and soft, and is accompanied by a strong odor of decay. It is caused by little or no care of the hoofs and lack of sanitary conditions in the stall. It can be avoided by keeping the stall clean and by using the hoof-pick regularly to remove packed manure from your horse's hoofs. The condition needs constant and often prolonged treatment, under the direction of your veterinarian, of course.

Founder is an inflammation of the sensitive part of the hoof's interior. It is caused by injury to the blood vessels of one or more feet, usually the front ones. The disease can be caused by overeating, drinking cold water, improper cooling out after hard exercise, or fast riding on a hard surface.

A foundered horse will experience intense pain and the affected feet will be hot and sensitive to the touch. Temperature may go as high as 106° F. (41.1 C.) and the patient will break out in a heavy sweat. The

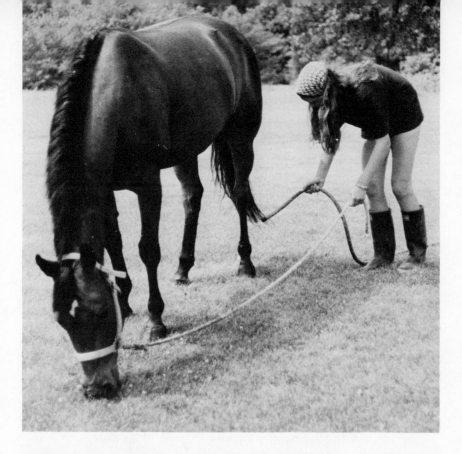

*Swelling in a leg or heat in a hoof caused by foundering can
be relieved with cool water from a hose or by having the horse
stand in a stream until the vet arrives*

damage to the feet will be permanent, with a wrinkling or series of rings on
the front wall of the foot.

Apply wet cold packs to the feet, or stand your horse in a cool stream
until the vet arrives. Special trimming and corrective shoeing will probably
be needed after the disease has been brought under control.

Other sources of lameness include a stone lodged in the foot, over-
work, bad shoeing, strains, bruises, infection, scratches in the backs of the
pasterns (similar to chapped hands), bowed tendons, quarter crack of the
hoof, navicular disease, hock ailments, and shoe boils. Your horse should
not be ridden until the condition is pinpointed and corrected.

Determine which leg is affected by trotting the horse on hard ground.
He will raise his head when the bad foot goes down to take weight off the
injured leg, usually a front one. Clean out the sore foot to see if there is a
stone, nail, or piece of glass causing the trouble.

If your horse has been shod within the last three days, you should have the shoe removed from the lame leg. A poorly placed nail may be causing the lameness.

Place your hands around the problem hoof and compare it with a hind foot to feel whether there is any heat in the wall of the hoof.

Next, go over the leg, working down from the elbow and looking for heat, swelling, or tenderness. If there is nothing that you can see, then the trouble may be in the shoulder or the stifle. Call your veterinarian for diagnosis and recommended treatment.

WORMS

Almost all animals have some worms, and horses have several different kinds, which, if kept in check by regular wormings, are not necessarily harmful. Like all parasites, however, worms do live at the expense of their host. The horse's condition will deteriorate if their numbers are allowed to multiply.

A horse with a serious worm problem will lose weight in spite of a good appetite, have a dull coat, constantly rub his tail, and will appear listless and generally unhealthy.

In addition to roundworms, pinworms, and bloodworms (the most dangerous), there is another common internal parasite—the larva of the horse botfly. The female fly lays her eggs on the horse's legs and underside of his body, where he can reach them with his mouth. They are licked up by the horse and hatch, eventually working their way to the digestive tract. The yellow eggs are found in clusters attached to the hair and can be removed by scraping (a hair-cutting instrument for family haircuts is easy to use) or washing away with hot water.

To prevent or control parasites in your barn, you should provide your horse with a clean stall, sanitary feed and water containers, and covered feed bins. Outside, you should:

have more than one pasture so you can practice rotation grazing,

not spread fresh manure in grazing fields,

pick up droppings in small paddocks,

have the manure pile removed regularly,

not allow horses to drink from barnyard puddles or to eat grain or hay from the ground where manure drainage and worms may contaminate them,

avoid overgrazing, because there are more parasites on the bottom inch of grass, and

keep pastures mowed to destroy the parasites' breeding and growing grounds.

Send a manure sample to your veterinarian in early spring and late fall, so the variety of worms and the degree of infestation can be determined. Worming medicines are highly poisonous, so have your vet do the worming rather than attempting it yourself with a commercial worming medicine.

OTHER HORSE DISEASES

The following partial list of diseases, with their causes, symptoms, treatments, and preventions, is only to supplement the services of your veterinarian and to aid you in recognizing an illness.

Azoturia affects the muscles of the loins and quarters.

Cause: Working an out-of-shape horse too hard or overfeeding a well-conditioned horse without giving the usual exercise.

Treatment: Stop working the horse immediately and keep him warm and quiet, with a blanket over the loins.

Prevention: Warm your horse up gradually. Feed him according to the amount of work he is doing and exercise him regularly.

Encephalomyelitis, or sleeping sickness, is caused by viruses that are carried from infected areas to clean ones by mosquitoes and birds. The two most common forms are the Eastern and Western strains. An outbreak of Venezuelan equine encephalomyelitis (VEE) occurred in Texas in 1971, but none has been reported since. The Eastern and VEE forms of the disease are almost always fatal. VEE is contagious to humans, too.

Symptoms: Sleepy appearance, wandering aimlessly and without coordination, grinding of teeth, inability to swallow, standing with head down, and even blindness. Infected animals either recover or die in two to four days.

Treatment: A veterinarian should be called at once, because serum is sometimes effective if given early enough. Good nursing, with possible forced feeding and watering, will aid your horse's recovery.

Prevention: Mosquitoes should be controlled by keeping barn and pastures well drained, and all horses should be vaccinated before May of each year or when the disease makes its appearance in your area.

Equine infectious anemia, or swamp fever, is an infectious viral disease spread by any bloodsucking insect, particularly stable flies.

Symptoms: High and intermittent fever; stiffness and weakness, especially in the hindquarters; anemia; loss of weight but not loss of appetite; and swelling of the lower body and legs. Most infected animals die within two to four weeks, but some horses recover and are carriers for the rest of their lives. They should be destroyed to protect others.

Prevention: Practice good sanitation to reduce the number of biting insects and have your horse tested (Coggins) annually for infection.

Heaves is similar to asthma in humans and is an incurable respiratory ailment that comes on very slowly over a long period of time.

Symptoms: A deep, hacking cough, difficulty in breathing with a whistling or wheezing sound when the horse inhales, and shortness of wind. The horse's flanks will heave even after mild exertion, and every attack causes additional damage to the air sacs in the lungs.

Treatment: A horse that develops the heaves must be rested immediately or the condition could be fatal. Avoid dusty hay and dusty trails. Wet your hay and grain down and use a cough medicine prescribed by your vet, who may also tell you to substitute pellet concentrates and other special feeds for hay. Avoid long, hard periods of exercising, but slowly try to get your horse in condition to be used for nearby trail rides and mild ring work.

Prevention: There is no prevention, but with proper care the condition can be relieved if not too far developed.

Tetanus, or lockjaw, is caused by bacteria that enter the body, usually through a wound. Death occurs in over 50 percent of the cases and tetanus affects all ages.

Symptoms: The first sign of the disease is a stiffness about the head. The horse chews slowly and swallows with difficulty. Next, the third or inner eyelid protrudes over the eyeball, and the slightest movement or noise starts violent spasms in the affected horse. Usually, the patient will continue standing almost until death.

Treatment: Call your vet immediately to give the wounded animal an injection of antiserum. It must be administered within 72 hours after the injury. The sick horse should be kept as quiet and as comfortable as possible with plenty of water and soft feed available.

Prevention: The stable area should be kept clean and tetanus toxoid given in two doses at six-week intervals by your veterinarian. Booster shots should then be given annually.

TEETH

Teeth are very important to a horse's well-being. Unhealthy, irregular teeth may cause the horse to swallow food whole, so it passes right through the digestive system, or he may drop food while chewing. Both may result in problems of nutrition.

All horses wear their teeth down through chewing, but, unlike human teeth, horses' molars keep on growing until the horse is quite old. As the softer cement surfaces of the teeth wear away through constant grinding, sharp points of hard enamel protrude to keep the surface rough for grinding. Sometimes these sharp points poke painfully into the opposite gums, and the horse cannot eat without considerable pain. The animal may also react quite negatively to any bit put in the mouth, constantly champing on it and tossing his head.

To correct these too-sharp surfaces, your veterinarian or a horse dentist should check your horse's teeth once a year and, if necessary, "float" or file them down.

BANDAGING

Leg bandages may be used to give support to a leg by reinforcing weak tendons, for leg protection on a horse that is being vanned to another destination and will be standing for a long period of time, or to cover a wound.

Bandages differ in materials used and ways of applying, according to

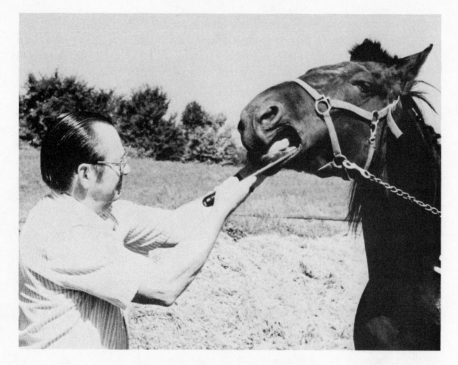

Your horse's teeth should be checked annually and may need to be "floated" or filed

their purpose, but all have some do's and don'ts.

Do put your horse in crossties before beginning to wrap.

Don't sit down on the floor.

Do crouch down as you wrap, so you can move out of the way if the horse kicks.

Don't wrap without first applying a thick layer of cotton for cushioning around the leg.

Do make the bandage only tight enough to stay in place.

Don't stop the circulation.

Do wrap the bandage smoothly, following the contours of the leg.

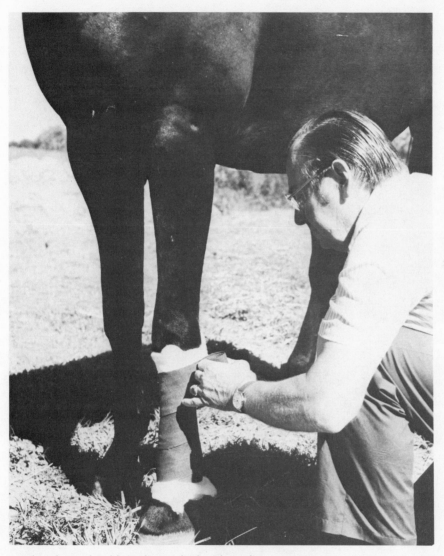

*Leg bandages should not be applied without first wrapping a
thick layer of cotton for cushioning around the leg*

Don't wrap over the knee.

Do start at the top of the area you wish to wrap, work down, and then back to the top, where you can tie the two ends together in a bow.

Don't end with a knot that is too difficult to undo quickly.

Do tie or fasten the bandage on the outside of the leg, not the inside, front or back.

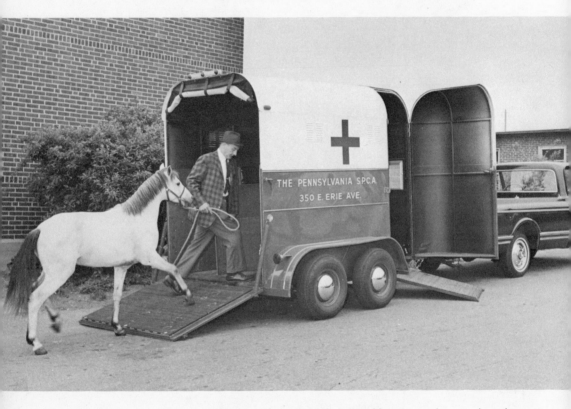

A very sick or severely injured horse may have to be taken to an equine clinic for treatment

CALLING YOUR VETERINARIAN

Horses can become infected with many of the same diseases that people get—glaucoma, sinusitis, heart failure, rhinitis, and pneumonia, among them. When you call the veterinarian about your sick horse, you should be prepared to give all the information requested, just as teen-agers or their parents do when they call their family physician.

Calmly give an accurate description of your horse's symptoms—if he is standing or can't get up, if he is eating and eliminating normally, if he has a temperature, or if the wound (in case of one) is bleeding, swelling, etc.

When your veterinarian does arrive, stay out of the way during the examination. If the vet asks you to hold your horse, try to keep him as still as possible by reassuring with your voice and your hands. If the veterinarian is unable to make a complete examination because your horse is too excited, a nose clamp or twitch may be used. It may look cruel to you, but, remember, it is only being used for the good of your horse's health. Be sure to follow faithfully all of your veterinarian's instructions regarding medication and treatment.

A great majority of all calls made by veterinarians are the result of carelessness on the part of horse owners. To cut down on your horse's medical care—and even eliminate almost all but the annual boosters and vaccinations—you should feed your horse a well-balanced diet in clean sanitary facilities; try to control the parasites around the stable and pasture area; keep your horse outdoors as much as possible; and exercise and groom him daily.

10
HORSE SHOWS AND GYMKHANAS

Small horse shows and gymkhanas can be all-day outings for the entire family: trailers and station wagons parked around the ring or in the shade under nearby trees; picnic lunches served on tail gates or spread out on blankets; horses everywhere—chestnuts, bays, blacks, and grays; and everyone participating either as competitor, photographer, groom, or spectator.

Local events, usually one-day affairs, can be found somewhere in your area almost every weekend throughout the summer months. Your neighborhood tack shop or riding stable will have brochures on the upcoming events, and information is also listed in local newspapers. Once you have shown a few times you will probably be put on a mailing list and receive advance notification at home.

You will meet many of the same riders and their families again and again as you make the rounds of these smaller horse shows and gymkhanas, and you will have an excellent opportunity to make new friends with a common interest—horses.

The spring shows are exciting for everyone, but as the summer progresses, the weekly or biweekly hassle becomes tedious. By fall, parents, riders, and horses are exhausted. However, after a few months of winter's solitude, memories and friendships from the past summer will rekindle the flames of competition once again and you will hardly be able to wait for the next show season to begin.

HORSE SHOWS

American Horse Shows Association (AHSA) events are "recognized" shows. Records of the results of their AHSA point classes are kept so that competitors can accumulate points for end-of-the-season awards and for eligibility to enter large shows such as the Devon Horse Show in Pennsylvania or the National Horse Show in Madison Square Garden in New York City. Riders trying to win these high point AHSA trophies must show just about every weekend in spite of the weather or the way they feel, and since classes can be open to anyone under eighteen, a ten-year-old may have to compete against a rider several years older.

The American Quarter Horse Association and other breed associations, such as the Appaloosa Horse Club and the Morgan Horse Club, sponsor shows to maintain the high quality of their particular breed by judging the entrants' ability and conformation.

Other organizations, such as 4-H Clubs, Pony Clubs, fraternal organizations, and charities, sponsor "unrecognized" shows held at local riding stables, fairgrounds, or in the open fields of someone's farm or estate. "Unrecognized" shows are often smaller and more fun, with less tension than the larger ones, although the competition here can still be quite stiff.

Recognized shows have entry fees of from $4 to $15 for each class, which often must be mailed in advance. For most small shows, entry fees start at $2 (some have just a fee for the day no matter how many classes you enter) and go up no higher than $4. They are usually paid to a secretary at the judge's stand when you arrive on the day of the show. You may also be asked to sign a statement at this time releasing the show's sponsor and property owners from responsibility if you or your horse is injured.

Horse shows have three types of classes—equitation or horsemanship classes, pleasure horse and hunter classes, and jumping classes.

Equitation or horsemanship classes judge the riders—hands, seat, and control of their mounts at various gaits or over a jump course and general poise and gracefulness. In pleasure horse and hunter classes the horse is judged for performance, conformation, way of going, manners, suitability, and soundness. Jumping classes are judged solely on the horse's ability to clear designated jumps, whether trotting or galloping around the course. Scoring is on a mathematical basis. A hind foot touching or "ticking" a jump counts half a fault, a front foot one fault, knockdowns by hind or front feet two and four faults respectively, and a third refusal, not following the proper course, or falling by either the horse or the rider as immediate elimination.

Some horse shows use the democratic Danish system of judging in which a rider competes, in effect, against herself. In any one given class there might be five blue (first) ribbons awarded or none at all. In another, everyone might get a red (second) or yellow (third) ribbon.

The most familiar type of evaluation is one in which the judges pick the best, second best, etc., in the class against an ideal that they have in their minds. The riders are supposed to be faceless and nameless to the judge. "Ribbons" are the rosettes pinned on the winners' bridles. In addition to the first three colors there are white (fourth), pink (fifth), green (sixth), purple (seventh), and brown (eighth). All classes award five ribbons except for the stake classes, which give out eight.

Equitation or horsemanship classes, either Western or English, judge the rider's hands, seat, and control of her mount

GYMKHANAS

A gymkhana consists of "games on horseback," a kind of field day of fun events. These classes are particularly good for riders with limited riding experience, but, although very informal, they do start you off on a whole new experience as a horse owner. Gymkhana riders compete against the clock as well as each other. The fastest time without a fault, such as knocking over a pole or stepping on the keyhole's limed lines, wins first prize.

Gymkhanas may also be "recognized" if they are members of the gymkhana division of the AHSA. A new addition to the traditional horse show world, AHSA Gymkhanas have stricter rules than those in the sport's previous years. Bats, quirts, and crops are now forbidden, and tie-downs are restricted. The reasons for these and other changes in the rules were primarily for the rider's safety and the humane handling of the horses. It used to be a common occurrence to see riders beat their mounts the entire way around a timed event's course. The length of tie-downs is checked, because if they are too short, they can cause a horse to lose his balance and possibly fall on the rider.

The classes included in the AHSA Gymkhana rules are the cloverleaf barrel race, quadrangle stake race, pole bending, relay race, rescue competition, keyhole, speed barrel competition, figure-eight stake, and the scurry (where a horse must go over three low jumps).

Other fun events are musical bags, egg and spoon, dollar bareback (in which you must not let a dollar bill slip out from between your knee and the horse's side while walking, trotting, and cantering bareback), Simon Says, and costume competition. In this last class both horse and rider must be in costume.

WHY AND WHAT TO ENTER

Horse shows and gymkhanas are excellent measuring sticks of your and your horse's ability to work together as a team in competition with others. Whether you are jumping your horse two feet six inches, signaling to begin a collected canter, or urging on during a barrel race, the two of you should be partners, competing as one.

This partnership can hardly be formed in a day or two, but must be built up over weeks of conditioning and practicing together. Find out what to practice by selecting the classes you wish to enter in an upcoming show and read up on their requirements. If it is a walk, trot, and canter horsemanship class, you should walk, trot on both diagonals, and canter in both leads at home until both of you can perform them perfectly together. One class may include dismounting and backing up, while another may add the hand gallop to its requirements, so you should always be prepared for a judge's request.

A current book on AHSA classes may be obtained from the American Horse Shows Association, 527 Madison Avenue, New York, N.Y. 10022.

Your riding ability, your horse's or pony's training, and whether you ride English or Western will determine what classes are best for you. Go to a few nearby shows to see what the participants are asked to do in the classes you are interested in entering, and study the winners to see what they are doing to win. You are paying for a judge's opinion, so be sure you are in the right class with every chance at winning. Your riding instructor or a knowledgeable friend or parent (knowledgeable when it comes to assessing your horsemanship and your horse's ability for a particular class's requirements) can help you with this choice. Do not make the mistake of entering too many classes (3 to 5 is the maximum) or you will only wear out your horse. Your pet will be full of vim in the morning but pooped out by the afternoon, so take this into consideration when deciding what classes to enter and the time of day they are scheduled.

TRANSPORTATION

If you don't own a trailer, make arrangements well in advance for a friend to pick you and your horse up (you pay for the gas) or for a local rental firm or stable to transport your horse to the show. Depending on the distance you will be traveling, the vanning fee is usually $10 to $15.

If you live near the showgrounds, you can hack over, but be sure to arrive early enough for your horse to rest up before the first class. If the trip is a long one, you may want to arrive the day before and stable your horse overnight. Be sure to make reservations early enough.

SHOW PREPARATION

For your horse's safety, be sure the animal has had all inoculations and a current Coggins test for equine infectious anemia. This last test is sometimes required for entrance into a show, but if not, have it done anyway. You may think that certainly entrants in horse shows are healthy —and they may even look that way to you—but there are carriers of disease even in the horse world. As an extra precaution, do not stand your horse next to another and allow them to rub noses. Do not let him drink from a public watering trough, or even graze where another horse has. Keeping your horse off in a corner, far away from any other horses, is a good idea, but hardly foolproof. Remember that even children wandering around the showgrounds, going from horse to horse, petting each one, can spread germs.

Set aside a definite time every day when you and your horse can practice. This will get both of you in condition as well as familiarize you with the routines of the classes you will be entering. Do not make these sessions too long or your horse will become bored. Several half-hour practices are better than one three-hour marathon. Vary the exercises. If you are planning to enter a jumping class, do not overjump your horse and make him weary of the whole idea.

If possible, try to get some instruction from a professional, not an interested friend or a patronizing parent, to at least give you hints on how to show your particular horse to his best ability. A knowledgeable instructor on the sidelines can see and tell you what you are doing wrong much more accurately than you can judge from the back of the horse.

If your horse acts up when other horses are around and you are planning on entering a horsemanship class where there will be plenty of company, invite some of your friends to bring their horses over or you jog to a nearby stable. Then practice the various gaits in a ring with horses alongside you, behind you, passing you, etc., so your mount becomes familiar with show-ring procedure.

To accustom your horse to traffic, you could lead him along a not too heavily traveled road, stand him next to the driveway and have someone drive the car back and forth, or turn him out in a field next to a road.

A horse that is not well mannered at home will be worse in a show, so do not go expecting improvement. The highly charged atmosphere of a show-ring puts even well-trained, steady horses on edge.

A good rider has complete control over the horse without a lot of shouting, arm-waving, and whip-slashing. If you find yourself losing your temper, stop for the day, even if you have not worked together for the allotted time you set aside. Patience and understanding will go a long way toward correcting any bad habits or poor training your horse may have, but do not expect miracles overnight. Training and conditioning always take time.

For the best results, schooling should be done in an enclosed ring or field. Always shut the gate to prevent your horse from ducking out. Rather than going over and over the walk, trot, and canter, try figure eights at a trot and then a canter, making sure to change leads in the center.

Trot or canter and practice stopping to an absolute standstill. Trot over poles laid on the ground, back through two posts, and open and shut gates from your horse's back. Try sitting at a trot and then attempt all three gaits without stirrups. Do a portion of your training and conditioning on the trails as a welcome break from the unavoidable drudgery that ring work can become, but do not relax to the point of sloppiness. It contributes to bad form and poor habits in both of you.

JUMPING

If you are planning on entering a jumping class, start your horse slowly at home over low, uncomplicated jumps and work up to higher, more unusual obstacles, such as trash cans, hedges, tree trunks, and wildly painted barrels. Provide as many jumping experiences as possible, so your horse will not shy at anything in the ring. Jumps should be sturdy but collapsible, so if your horse hits a bar, it will fall rather than trip him.

Start jumping with wings if your horse runs out of the jump instead of going over, and remove them once he gets the idea.

Always wear a hard hat when jumping and never keep your balance by hanging on to the reins. Instead, grab a handful of mane or the martingale if the horse overjumps. Look over the course you will be following and memorize the sequence of jumps you are to take. One mistake will eliminate you from the class.

THE DAY BEFORE THE SHOW

For the last few weeks you should have been giving special attention to your horse's coat, mane, and tail so they now have a natural sheen. The day before the show give a thorough cleaning—trimming, pulling the mane and tail, and putting in a little extra scrubbing on those white socks.

Always wear a hard hat when jumping and never hang on to the reins for balance

For a white tail stained with manure and dirt, use a little diluted bleach on the ends to whiten them.

If you are going to braid mane and tail, sponge them first, because wet hair is easier to plait. Use strong thread or yarn to hold the braids in place.

Put a sheet or light blanket on your horse for the night and keep him in the stall with extra bedding to prevent lying down in any mud or manure.

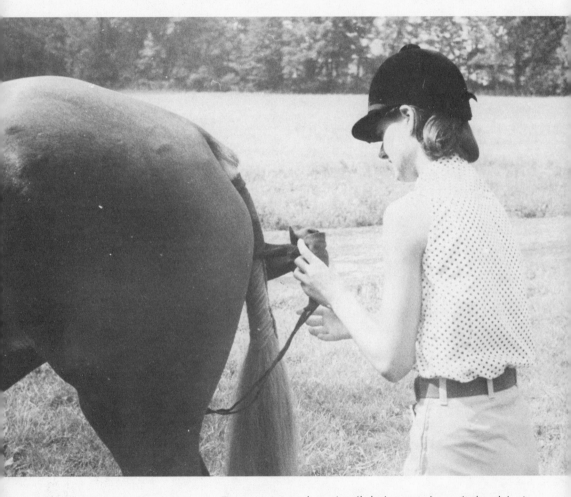

To protect your horse's tail during vanning, wind a plain Ace bandage around it

As you enter the ring remember you are out to win, but do not forget courtesy and the rights of other competitors

A few stains and smudges are unavoidable, but they can be quickly touched up in the morning.

Clean your tack and lay out your own clothes. Try to look your best, eye-catching but not gaudy. You will have a much wider choice of colors and styles if you are dressing in Western clothes than in the conservative English style.

Try to have colors of hat, shirt, and pants complement you and your horse. No red on a chestnut (too blah), but by all means, wear it on a black or gray horse for a striking combination.

Your hair should be neat and tucked in under your hat for the show. If it is long, put it in a braid, bun, or hairnet for the event, because if your hair is flopping, you will look as if you are, too.

A clean, shiny horse and a neat, coordinated outfit are attributes against any riding competitor.

SHOW TIME

On the morning of the show, get up early and, wearing old clothes, water and feed your horse. After your breakfast, muck out the stall, put down a thick layer of clean bedding, remove the blanket, brush out any night stains, pick out feet and polish hoofs with dressing. To protect your horse's tail during vanning, wind a plain Ace bandage from the top down to just above the end of the tailbone, and pin or tie it on the outside.

Although show day may appear to be bright and sunny, experienced showgoers will bring umbrellas and other rain gear along with their folding chairs, blankets, and sunshades.

In addition to saddle, bridle, halter, and lead shank, you should bring your own grooming equipment—brushes, currycomb, old terry cloth, and, most important of all, a hoof-pick—for last-minute and periodic touch-ups during the day. An extra lead shank and halter will be greatly appreciated if one gets lost, broken, or stolen. Hay for your horse to nibble on throughout the day and your own water are two other items to remember.

Even though the show's brochure states that water is available, some horses are particularly fussy if it has a different taste or odor, and lugging a bucket or two of sloshing water from the end of the showgrounds where the water is located to your trailer is hardly the way to keep yourself looking cool and clean. Bring extra clothing in case an accident soils your original outfit.

A light sheet is essential to protect a sweating horse from drafts, and

*If your horse refuses a jump, never show your temper, but try
again to take him over it*

it will also keep him cleaner. Fly spray or wipe will drive off many of the flies that can irritate an already nervous horse to distraction, and a first-aid kit for you and your horse is a good item to add to your gear, too.

Arrive at the showgrounds in plenty of time to park in a convenient spot, pay your entry fee, and pick up your number. Give your horse water and hay immediately, but take it away an hour before your first class.

Acquaint your horse with the new surroundings. Hubbub, crowds, other horses, and unfamiliar objects may be quite frightening at first, so you want the animal to get accustomed to all this before you are under a judge's scrutiny. If you have entered a jumping class, let your horse watch the jumps being set up.

You will not be allowed to school in the main ring or over fences on the outside course if it is being used, but a horse that is unusually full of energy can let off some steam in the schooling ring or other areas set aside for exercising. Give him time to cool off and relax before your first class.

FIRST CLASS

When your class is called, mount up and give your boots one last flick of the dust cloth before entering the ring. Ring manners impress judges. Keeping a judge waiting while you saddle up when you should already be in the ring is a strike against you. As you enter the ring, go to your right and walk your horse counterclockwise close to the rail.

You are out to win and should use everything you know to achieve this goal, but do not forget courtesy and the rights of other competitors. Try to stay as calm and relaxed as possible, because your reins will act as telegraph wires and send every insecure signal to your horse. Your body should be flexible and supple, moving with your horse in all gaits. Be aware of the signals the horse gives you (pawing and fidgeting if nervous and excited, ears back if annoyed), so you can anticipate and correct any sudden move. If your mount starts to act up, pull out of line until you can quiet him. If he continues to misbehave, you will have to leave the ring so as not to jeopardize another's performance.

Be an individual and show your horse to his best advantage. Ride him the way he goes best, not necessarily the way the rest of the class is going. If he has a smooth fast trot, let him trot on, even if you do pass the rest of the horses. However, you decide, not the horse. You be the boss.

Experienced competitors will give their horses plenty of room in which to work, avoiding ring congestion for several reasons. Most important of all is the safety factor. All horses have the potential to kick if crowded. Another possible hazard is that other horses may affect your own mount's performance, with such moves as stopping suddenly in front of you just as you are passing in front of the judge in a collected canter. The judge will obviously get a better look at you and your horse if you are not crammed into a hodgepodge of horseflesh and other riders.

Slower horses should stay on the rail, so that the faster ones can pass on the inside.

If you find yourself boxed in, make a small circle at one end of the ring and move into line in an open area. You can also lose ground to the horses surrounding you by staying to the outside at the arena's ends (most horses take the shortcut across them) or gain ground by cutting off the ends completely. The ideal place is on the rail, with no other horses overlapping you.

When you are asked for another gait, make the change a smooth one with as little motion as possible. Your horse should be on the proper lead when asked to canter. If he is not, stop immediately and start him again until he is, even if you happen to be in front of the judge. This will make a better impression than continuing on the wrong lead.

Do not try to correct every little thing your horse does wrong. Your homework should be done at home, not in the show-ring. Even if your horse is cantering in double time, give him a loose rein and keep a smile on your face as you pass the judges so they will think you are in complete control. However, once out of their line of vision, take immediate action by pulling your horse back. Never show your temper or hit your horse. Both judges and spectators will disapprove.

If you have entered the pole-bending event in a gymkhana, do not wear chaps or a wide hat. Either one can knock over a pole if you ride too close. Loose, flapping straps are also a hazard. Be sure your hat fits so that it does not fly off or fall down over your eyes. A pole is a lot easier to knock down than a barrel, particularly the end poles. Your horse must be trained not to get too close to them.

If you fall off, hang on to your reins and get up as quickly as you can to let everyone know that you are not hurt. Later, try not to hash over the incident with everyone. Just push it aside as another experience you hope not to repeat.

When the judge asks that all the horses be lined up in the center of the ring for inspection at the end of the class, try to keep five feet between your horse and the ones on each side.

If you are not picked as a winner, congratulate those who have been

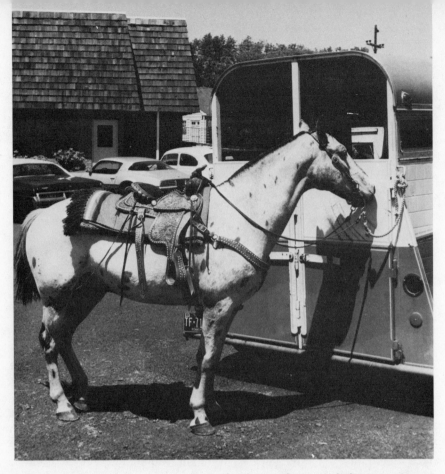

Never leave your horse tied alone at your van

and plan on doing better next week. Winning is an obvious desire of every competitor, but it should not overshadow everything else. Showing should be fun, and sportsmanship a part of horsemanship. If you have trained and conditioned both yourself and your horse to the best of your ability, and performed well during the class, then that is all you can ask. The winner of a class is the best in one judge's opinion, and what one judge may dislike in one class could very well appeal to another judge in the next. Do not get discouraged. It may be you and your horse that will be "pinned" next week.

AFTER COMPETITION

In between classes allow your horse to rest. Never leave him tied alone at the van or car. If you take your mount with you to watch some of the other classes, give his back a rest, do not use it as a grandstand seat.

If this was your lucky day, remember that being a good winner is as important as being a good loser

Allow your horse to rest in between classes. Never use his back as a grandstand seat

Loosen the girth a few notches, remembering to tighten it again before mounting. Do not lead your horse near parked cars, jostle other spectators, or allow all your friends to take quick turns around the practice ring. Instead, spend your time wisely by watching other riders and learning what the judge is looking for. Try to pick out the winners in each class before they are announced.

After the show is over, get your horse home as quickly as possible. Trying to unload and take care of a tired horse in the dark is no fun if you are exhausted too. Make sure he has fresh thick bedding. Groom him thoroughly and unbraid mane and tail to prevent the hairs from splitting. Give a good feed and leave water and hay for the night.

The constant round of shows and gymkhanas may eventually sour your horse on them, so follow a weekend of competition with a good rest.

If this did happen to be your lucky day and all your hard work paid off, remember that being a good winner is just as important as being a good loser.

APPENDIX
HORSE PUBLICATIONS

AMERICAN HORSEMAN
Countrywide Communications, Inc.
222 Park Avenue South
New York, N.Y. 10003

AMERICAN SHETLAND PONY JOURNAL
Box 2339
West Lafayette, Ind. 47906

APPALOOSA HORSE NEWS
Box 403
Moscow, Idaho 83843

ARABIAN HORSE WORLD
2650 East Bayshore
Palo Alto, Calif. 94303

BACKSTRETCH, THE
19363 James Couzens Highway
Detroit, Mich. 48235

CHRONICLE OF THE HORSE
Middleburg, Va. 22117

CLASSIC
551 Fifth Avenue
New York, N.Y. 10017

EQUESTRIAN TRAILS
10723 Riverside Drive
North Hollywood, Calif. 91602

HORSE AND HORSEMAN
P.O. Box HH
Capistrano Beach, Calif. 92624

HORSE AND RIDER
Box 4038
Covina, Calif. 91723

HORSE LOVER'S NATIONAL MAGAZINE
651 Braman Street
San Francisco, Calif. 94107

HORSE LOVER MAGAZINE, THE
Box 914
El Cerrito, Calif. 94530

HORSE, OF COURSE!
Derbyshire Building
Temple, N.H. 03084

HORSE PLAY MAGAZINE
50-B Ridge Road
Greenbelt, Md. 20770

HORSE TALES
Western Publications, Inc.
P.O. Box 3338
Austin, Tex. 78764

HORSE WORLD
P.O. Box 588
Lexington, Ky. 40501

HORSEMAN, THE MAGAZINE OF WESTERN
RIDING
5314 Bingle Road
Houston, Tex. 77018

HORSEMEN'S YANKEE PEDLAR
Box 897
Wilbraham, Mass. 01095

MORGAN HORSE, THE
Box 265
West Lake Moraine Road
Hamilton, N.Y. 13346

NATIONAL HORSEMAN, THE
933 Baxter Avenue
Louisville, Ky. 40204

NORTHEAST HORSEMAN
Box 47 Summer Street
Hampden Highlands, Maine 04445

PAINT HORSE JOURNAL, THE
P.O. Box 12487
Fort Worth, Tex. 76116

PALOMINO HORSES
Box 249
Mineral Wells, Tex. 76067

PINTO HORSE
P.O. Box 3984
San Diego, Calif. 92103

PRACTICAL HORSEMAN
Pennsylvania Horse, Inc.
19 Wilmot Mews
West Chester, Pa. 19380

QUARTER HORSE JOURNAL
Box 9105
Amarillo, Tex. 79105

SADDLE AND BRIDLE
2333 Brentwood Boulevard
St. Louis, Mo. 63144

SOUTHERN HORSEMAN, THE
P.O. Box 5735
Meridian, Miss. 39301

WELSH NEWS
1770 Lancaster Avenue
Paoli, Pa. 19301

WESTERN HORSEMAN, THE
3580 North Nevada Avenue
Colorado Springs, Colo. 80907

U.S. DEPARTMENT OF AGRICULTURE
Superintendent of Documents
U.S. Government Printing Office
Washington, D.C. 20402
    Agricultural Handbook No. 394,
        Breeding and Raising Horses
    Agricultural Handbook No. 353,
        Horsemanship and Horse Care
    Stock Number 0100–02812, *Horse
        Safety Guidelines*

Horse Associations

American Buckskin Registry Association
P.O. Box 1125
Anderson, Calif. 96007

American Horse Protection Association, Inc.
%Mrs. William L. Blue
3316 N Street, N.W.
Washington, D.C. 20007

American Paint Horse Association
P.O. Box 12487
Fort Worth, Tex. 76116

American Quarter Horse Association
P.O. Box 200
Amarillo, Tex. 79105

American Shetland Pony Club
P.O. Box 2339
West Lafayette, Ind. 47902

Appaloosa Horse Club, Inc.
Box 403
Moscow, Idaho 83843

Arabian Horse Club Registry of America
One Executive Park
7801 Belleview Avenue
Englewood, Colo. 80110

International Arabian Horse Assn.
224 East Olive Avenue
Burbank, Calif. 91503

International Buckskin Horse Registry
P.O. Box 2194
Redding, Calif. 96001

Morgan Horse Club, Inc.
P.O. Box 2157
West Hartford, Conn. 06117

National Pony Club Secretary
Pleasant Street
Dover, Mass. 02030

Palomino Horse Association
Box 446
Chatsworth, Calif. 91311

Pinto Horse Association of America
Box 3984
San Diego, Calif. 92103

Pony of the Americas Club, Inc.
P.O. Box 1447
Mason City, Iowa 50401

Welsh Pony Society of America
202 North Chester Street
West Chester, Pa. 19308

GLOSSARY

aged   a horse nine years of age or older

Appaloosa   a breed of horse developed by the Nez Percé Indians, with black and white spotted markings on the rump and loins

Arabian   a breed of horses that originated in Arabia

bay   horse with any shade of brown coat and black mane, tail, lower legs

broomtails   wild Western horses

buckskin   a tan horse with a black mane, tail, and legs and a stripe along the spine

cast   a horse that lies or falls down and cannot get up without help is said to be "cast"

chaps   seatless overalls made of leather and worn over jeans for protection when riding through brush or in cold weather

Coggins test   a blood test to detect the presence of the virus that produces equine infectious anemia, commonly called swamp fever

cold blood or **crossbred**   a horse with parents of different breeds

collected   alert, with feet properly under

colt   a male horse or pony that is past the age of being nursed but under four years of age

conformation   the muscle and bone structure forming the shape or outline of a horse; the way a horse is put together

cribbing   biting or setting the teeth against a wooden object, such as a fence or manger, while sucking air into the lungs

dam   the female parent of a horse

dobbin   a gentle, old horse

dressage   the advanced training of a horse, in which he performs certain difficult steps and gaits according to very slight movements of his rider

141

equestrian   a skilled rider of horses

equine   of or pertaining to a horse

equitation   the art of riding a horse

filly   a young female horse or pony up to four years of age

fit   in top condition

five-gaited   trained to perform five gaits: walk, trot, canter, "slow-gait," and rack

foal   a horse or pony from birth until he stops nursing

frog   the triangular horny pad on the bottom of a horse's foot

gait   the way of moving, such as walk, trot, canter, jog, etc.

gelding   a male horse castrated or neutered by surgery so he cannot be bred

grade horse   a horse or pony that is not of any breed

green horse   one with little training

groom   to clean and brush a horse, or one who cleans horses

horsemanship   the skill involved in riding and caring for a horse

jog   a slow, steady trot

lead shank   a rope or line attached to a halter for the purpose of leading a horse

light horse   any horse used for riding or driving; not a draft breed, such as a Percheron or a Clydesdale

Lipizzans   an all-white breed of horse trained by the Spanish Riding School in Vienna, Austria, for dressage exhibitions

longeing cavesson   a special halter with a swivel ring on the top of the noseband or cavesson for longeing

mare   a female horse or pony over four years of age

muck out   to clean a horse's stall of manure and soiled bedding

mustangs   wild horses

navicular disease   a disease involving the bones inside a horse's foot

neat's-foot oil   a leather dressing made from bones of cattle

novice   an inexperienced or beginning rider

paddock   a small field or enclosure near the barn

paint or **pinto**   a horse with white and colored spots over the body

palomino   a golden or light-brown horse with a white or cream-colored mane and tail

piebald   a horse with black and white patches

pinned   winning a ribbon in a horse show

poncho   a cloaklike waterproof garment with a hole cut in the middle for the head

post   to rise and fall in the saddle in time to a horse's trot; an English style of riding

quarter horse   a chunky breed of horse that is known for its great bursts of speed up to a quarter of a mile

rallies   organized events to test riding skills

roached   a horse's mane cut short

roan   a solid color horse, such as reddish-brown, brown, or black, with a sprinkling of white hairs throughout

Roman nose   a nose that curves outward slightly

schooling   training a horse, especially over jumps

sheet   a light blanket to put on a sweating horse

Shetland   a breed of small, sturdy ponies

skewbald   a horse with patches of white and some color other than black

stallion   a male horse that has not been gelded and can be used for breeding purposes

thoroughbred   a breed of racehorses developed by crossing English mares with Arabian stallions

trailwise   steady, knowing the trails and unlikely to shy at strange objects

vice   any annoying habit that interferes with the horse's usefulness

weanling   a colt or filly between six months and one year of age

yearling   a colt or filly between one and two years of age

ACKNOWLEDGMENTS

Many friends—both those well acquainted with the world of horses and others who understood my needs as a writer—have supported or contributed to the writing of this book.

I am particularly indebted to Dr. Cameron Wilson, an avid fox hunter and very capable veterinarian who seems especially tuned in to the problems of his equine patients. In addition to assisting me with the information in various chapters, he was the one who originally gave me the idea to write about the backyard horse.

Other fellow horse lovers enthusiastically gave hours of their time to answer my questions, help with the photographs, and to read and reread parts of my manuscript, checking for accuracy. Listed in alphabetical order they are:

Kathy Carey	June Stefanelli
Carol Ann Craig	Barbara Ulmer
Jay Kennedy	Charles Wilson, D.D.S.
Anne Spurr	Daisy Windmassinger

Thanks, all of you.

INDEX

Strains, 109
Straw, 68, 80–81
Streams and puddles, 99–100
Stubbornness, 93
Sugar, 67
Suitability, 39
Supervision, 11–12
Supplies
  grooming, 70
  medical, 104–105
  miscellaneous, 71
  stall cleaning, 71
Swallow, inability to, 111, 113
Swamp fever, 112
Sweating, 107, 108, 128
Sweeping, 81
Sweet feed, 66
Swelling, 112
Symptoms, 117. *See also individual symptoms*

Tack (equipment), 41–58, 126
  inspection of, 96
Tack room, 19, 21, 56
Tail, 76–78, 94, 110, 126, 128
Talking to your horse, 71–72, 89, 92, 117
Teamwork, 121
Teeth, 89, 111, 113
Temperament, 35–36
Temperature (fever), 106, 107, 108
Tendons, bowed, 109
Terms of sale, 40
Tetanus (lockjaw), 104, 112–113
Throatlatch, 42
Thrush, 80, 108
Tourniquet, 106
Traffic, 99, 123
Trail riding, 95–103
Training (schooling), 39–40, 83
Trial period, 39
Tricks, 86
Transporting (vanning), 92–94, 122
Trimming
  hoofs, 80, 109
  mane, 78
Trot, 124, 130

Two-horse trailering, 93
Tying the horse, 103. *See also* Crossties

Unloading the van, 94
"Unrecognized" shows, 119
Uphill, riding, 100
Used tack, 53

Vacation care, 15
Vaccination, 104, 112
Vanning, 92–94, 122
VEE (Venezuelan equine encephalomyelitis), 111
Vein, cut, 106
Ventilation, 27
Veterinarian, 36, 38, 61, 104, 105, 107, 108, 110, 111, 112, 113, 117
  examination by, 38–39
Vices, 83, 85–91, 123, 131

Walking, 96–98, 103
Walking horse
  bit, 51
  bridle, 51
Walls, barn, 24–25
Wandering, aimless, 111
Warm-up, 81–82, 96, 98, 111
Warranty, 40
Watching the show, 134
Water, crossing, 99–100
Water equipment, 25, 26, 62, 110
Watering, 59, 61, 108, 123, 128, 130, 135
Weakness, 108, 112
Weaving, 86
Weight, 61–62, 110, 112
Western
  clothing, 55
  tack, 41–50
Weymouth bridle, 51
Wheelbarrow, 80
Whip, 51, 81, 82
Wind sucking, 86
Window guards, 22
Wings, 124
Winning, 131–132, 134